# THE TEN COMMANDMENTS

# The Ten Commandments
## Playing by the Rules

**Stuart Briscoe**

OM PUBLISHING
Carlisle, U.K.

Published by arrangement with
Harold Shaw Publishers,
Wheaton, Illinois, U.S.A.

This U.K. edition 1994

**British Library Cataloguing in Publication Data**

Briscoe, D. Stuart
  Ten Commandments: Playing by the Rules. – (Foundations of
  the Faith Series)
  I. Title II. Series
  248.4

ISBN 1-85078-145-1

OM Publishing is an imprint of Send the Light Ltd.,
PO Box 300, Carlisle, Cumbria, CA3 0QS, U.K.

Printed in the U.K. by Cox and Wyman Ltd., Reading.

# Contents

# Preface

Another book on the Ten Commandments?

Yes, and I'll tell you why! As I read a number of serious books on the subject, I found that most of them addressed issues of concern and interest in the day they were published but often said little or nothing about the issues we confront today. For instance one writer seemed desperately concerned about Sabbath keeping but said nothing about abortion or nuclear war—for the obvious reason that they were not problems at the time. This book attempts to apply the ancient Commandments to the modern era.

In addition, as I studied and meditated on the Commandments I talked with many people about them and discovered that though these people all revered them, they couldn't remember them! So I preached through them in the church I pastor and broadcast a series of television shows dealing with them. The response of many people was deep and lasting.

# Introduction

Suppose a friend invites you to a game one Sunday afternoon in the fall, telling you he has great tickets. You know one of your favorite teams will play football in your area, so you figure that's what he has in mind, even though he hasn't said so.

"Who's playing?" you ask.

"I don't know. They didn't tell me," your friend answers.

That sounds kind of odd, but he has a great sense of humor so you figure he wants to keep it as a surprise and just won't tell you now. You try to pump him. "Where will they play?"

"I thought we'd drive out to the big stadium," he tells you, and you're pretty sure you've figured out the surprise.

On Sunday you both arrive at the stadium, all psyched for a good game. Still your friend seems nervous about being in the right place and hasn't said much. So you ask the man next to you in line, "Who's playing?"

"They didn't say," he tells you.

That's funny! *Are we both supposed to be surprised?* you wonder.

Together you find your seats and ask around, but no one seems to know the answer. You begin to feel awfully confused.

Awhile later some activity starts down on the field, but you've never seen anything like it. People come out wearing all kinds of clothes, but no uniforms. Soon that doesn't seem to matter, though, because no one has a ball and no one pays any attention to the goal posts. Each person does just as he pleases. Some sit in the middle of the field, while others lie down on it. A few men run up and down, tripping on the prone and seated "players." But no one seems to know where to go or what to do. Several fellows seem to try to play one side and then the other.

Meanwhile, in the stands, some people boo softly, while others whisper a cheer. A man stands up and begins screaming for help, but everyone around him ignores him. Several people get into a fight, and no one pays any attention. Spectators sit or stand wherever they please, paying no attention to those trying to watch the field. Not long after, in frustration, you decide to go home.

That scenario sounds pretty silly, but I'd like to suggest that this crazy game reflects the state of our society. Today, playing by the rules isn't a popular idea. Look at the way we live—both individually and corporately.

First, you'll notice a prevailing sense of aimlessness in our communities. We lack a consensus of what we're about and of where we're going. Many varied opinions and philosophies tear us apart, until people often say, "Rules? Whose rules?" In addition, our society shows an intense distaste for anything authoritative—anything that tells us what we can do (or worse, what we can't do).

With our inordinate desire to be free to do exactly what we please, we naturally experience confusion in our society and our personal lives. Those who advocate no rules, no objectives for society, and would encourage us to do anything we want, anytime, anywhere, under any circumstances, condemn us to the same existence as one of the players in the stadium game without rules. Imagine yourself locked into this aimless, pointless game every day of your life. You probably don't have to imagine too hard, because many people recommend that kind of society today. We've seen the results.

The confusion, lack of aim, pointlessness, and hopelessness in our society relate directly to the lack of agreement that there even are principles or rules, things we should do and ways to do them. I believe that God, in the Ten Commandments, has succinctly spelled out some guidelines for us.

# Where Did the Commandments Come From?

God didn't suddenly lean out of heaven and zap Moses with the Ten Commandments. No, first he moved into the life of a man called Abraham. He spoke to Abraham and promised—made a covenant with him—that he would be the God of Abraham's descendants, the seed of Abraham, and that they would be God's people.

Abraham thought this was a rather strange covenant because at the time he was ninety-nine years old, and his wife, Sarah, was ninety; they had no children. When he told his wife about it, she went off into mild hysterics at the very idea. But God still stood by his promise, and as time went on Abraham and Sarah had a son. Then their son had a son, and eventually he had sons and sons and sons—and there you have the children of Israel.

The children of Israel went into Egypt and were taken captive by the Egyptians, and they had a terrible time as slaves down there. They wailed and bemoaned their fate, and they didn't really see how they were God's people at all—

God had promised them a land of their own, and they didn't have it. Where was the status he had promised them? They didn't have it! They were stuck in Egypt.

God heard their cry and raised up Moses. In a mass exodus under Moses' leadership, God brought the people out of Egypt, through the wilderness, and into the Promised Land. The Exodus dramatically demonstrated God's grace and power.

Three months after leaving Egypt, the people sat in the wilderness—not the most salubrious place. God called Moses to one side and told him to meet him on the mountain, while the people waited at the foot of the mountain. In his meeting with Moses, God renewed the covenant (Exod. 19:4-6), reaffirmed the special status of his people, and reminded them of the Promised Land. Again God assured them they were really his people, and he was really their God.

Then God told Moses, "On the basis of this renewed covenant, I want you to hear some instructions that you must take to the people." And God gave the Ten Commandments to Moses.

## What Does the Covenant Mean?

What was the point of these instructions? In Deuteronomy 6:5, forty years after the Exodus, Moses reminded the people of all these things. He made a great statement: "Love the LORD your God with all your heart and with all your soul and with all your strength." This command is a dominant theme of God's covenant with his people: He is their God, and they are his people. They share a love relationship.

I suspect that at some time a lot of earnest people have asked, "Excuse me, God, how do I love You?" The answer? You don't love God by having a fuzzy feeling, or by having a warm glow, or by having romantic thoughts. You love God by showing that he is supreme in your life, and you show that by doing what he says. So God gave the Ten Words, the Ten Instructions, and said, "If you want to know how to love me, do these things. Then you will be able to demonstrate your love." Having made the covenant, God spoke to Moses, saying, "The people want to know how to love me. Tell them how to do it. Give them the Ten Words."

If you check in Deuteronomy 10 and Leviticus 19, you find a second theme running through the covenant. Not only should God's people love him, they should love their neighbors as themselves. Now we have another question: "Excuse me, who is my neighbor, and what does it mean to love my neighbor? And how do I love myself?" The Ten Commandments were God's response to this question as well. These guidelines fill in the details of the "how to" of love. God offered a covenant of love and grace, and he amplified the loving relationship with the Ten Commandments.

Read Deuteronomy 6:2 and 18 and you'll discover that God also feels concerned about the community having what we might call "the good life." The Ten Commandments also form a "how-to" for developing the right kind of society. When people follow these covenant commands, they will begin to discover, to their amazement and delight, that they will have rich, full lives; their families will come together, and they will have an enriched society."

"How do we love God?"

"How do I love my neighbor?"

"How do we live the good life?"

The Ten Commandments show the way.

The Ten Commandments also offered the children of Israel a sense of what it means to be God's people as opposed to all the other nations about them. The other nations had laws, codes, and principles of operation. The Ten Commandments were the framework of laws, codes, and principles for God's chosen people.

## Terms of the Covenant

According to some recent research on ancient treaties in the Middle East, each little town had its own king. Sometimes the great king for the whole area would come along and clobber the smaller kingdoms, and the little kingdoms would end up as part of the larger territory of the more powerful king. When this happened, the great king would make a treaty with the smaller kings, which identified him as the *suzerain* and the smaller kings as the vassals. This treaty contained specific elements. First it told who the great king was and all about his power. The second part told how graciously and benevolently he had treated the little kings. The third part meticulously outlined how they were to live on the basis of this treaty. The fourth part ratified how it should be done, said where the copy of the treaty would be kept, and enunciated a proclamation about the treaty. The fifth part listed the blessings that would accrue to those who kept the treaty and the cursings for those who broke it. The sixth and final part invoked the gods of the nations involved to witness the signing of the treaty.

What relationship does this have to the Ten Commandments? The scholars who did this research discovered that when you compare Exodus and Deuteronomy to ancient treaties, you see that the Commandments fit into the same covenant form. In the case of the Commandments, God is the great king. The people of Israel are a kingdom of priests unto God—a nation. He states his benevolence toward them, stipulates the ten principles by which he expects them to live, and gives instructions about how he expects them to live on the basis of their covenant. All this formed their treaty with God.

## What about Us?

What do the Ten Commandments mean to us today? J. I. Packer describes today's moral and ethical thinking this way:

> We have assumed that self-exploration and self-discovery is a prime task, and any means to the end which does not violate others' freedom or destroy their well-being should be thought allowable, and the toleration of deviant behavior should be practiced up to the limit as being both a civilized virtue and a universal duty.

But how does that theory really work in society?

Suppose you decide to attend a symphony concert. You arrive at your local performing arts center and discover it's not the normal concert at all. You notice the timpani player seems to be having a clambake in his drum—clouds of steam curl up above it. That seems rather surprising, but even worse, the tuba player has cabbages and cauliflowers growing quite nicely in his instrument. Intriguingly, the harpist seems to have laundry draped over her harp.

The conductor comes on, notices all this, and insists that the three musicians clean up their act. "It won't do!" he tells them. "I will not tolerate this." So they get rid of the clambake, the vegetables, and the wash.

Everything's fine, right?

No, because they start to play, but as soon as the timpani player picks up his mallet, the trumpeter gets close to him and the drum player hits the fellow over the right ear with a resounding crack! This produces the wrong kind of sound. As the violinist brings her bow across her instrument, she sticks it right up the nose of the clarinetist.

The conductor says, "Come on now! Cut it out and get your act together."

Now everything should be okay. Right?

Not yet. The conductor raises his baton and the brass plays the Dead March, the woodwinds play a gavotte, and the strings play Viennese waltzes. Each of these is very beautiful, but together they are totally chaotic.

The conductors says, "Stop that! We'll play Beethoven's Ninth Symphony." Now the orchestra has a sense of direction. The conductor has sorted out the individual instruments; he's considered the relationship of one instrument to another; and he's developed a common theme.

Today's society says, "You don't need a common theme. We have to accept any kind of deviant behavior. Whatever you want to do is fine." But that's like letting the brass section play the Dead March while the other instruments play their favorite pieces. We can't go in every direction. Like the orchestra, we need a consensus. We need the theme the Ten Commandments provide. We flee from them at our peril.

# The Commandments and the Believer

This leads us to two questions. First: Do the Ten Commandments have any significance for believers? Some would say emphatically, "No! We're not under law, we're under grace." Others would respond, "Paul says that by observing the law no one will be justified. It's right here in Galatians 2:16. We don't even have to mention the Ten Commandments." They both say, "The Commandments have nothing to do with us today."

When Paul talks about the law in that passage in Galatians, he's addressing a particular problem of the church. He had gone into all kinds of areas of the world and had told the people, "You can't get right with God by living a good life because you can't live it good enough. If you admit you can't live it good enough, you will be open to God's forgiveness, not on your merits, but on the merits of Christ. You can be made right with God—justified—on the basis of God's free choice, not your merits; it comes by grace, by your receiving it freely through faith, not by your working at it." Paul gave this message. Lots of people believed.

Then the Judaizers came in and said, "Not so, Paul. Real believers adhere to all the meticulous details of the law." These guys didn't just mean the Ten Commandments. They meant over six hundred minute, nit-picking laws scholars had imposed on people. Really they meant, "You get right with God when you dot all your *i*'s and cross your *t*s and do absolutely everything absolutely right absolutely all the time."

Paul says, "No, we're not under that system at all. Even if we were, works of the law couldn't justify us. We're justified by grace through faith." But he's not saying, "Listen, believers, you're under grace; that means there aren't any rules; that means anything goes."

How do we know this? Because Jesus said, "I have not come to break the law, to destroy the law, I have come to fulfill it." The word *fulfill* means literally "to give full meaning." The Lord Jesus adhered to the Ten Commandments and was the living exposition of them. Moreover, Paul said that if we walk in the Spirit, we will fulfill the righteousness of the law.

Do the Ten Commandments have any significance for us today? Of course they do. Not as a means of *justification*, but as a means of *demonstrating* that we have been justified. You're not under law; you're under grace, in order that in the power of the Spirit you might fulfill the righteousness of the law as outlined in the Ten Commandments.

# The Commandments and the Unbeliever

"Do these laws have any relevance to unbelievers, too?" Our society comes up with all kinds of answers for this. Some say of the Commandments, "They're too simplistic. I won't accept them." Others say, "It's all relative. You need situational ethics here. One standard won't always work." A third group tells you, "The Commandments are too negative. I don't like them. Thou shalt not . . . Thou shalt not . . ." The free spirits say, "I have to be free to be me. There's no place for these outmoded, outrageous rules." Some folks have kind of given up as far as the Ten Commandments and unbelievers are concerned.

But look at your Bible, and you'll discover that long before God made the covenant with Abraham, he used the same principles in creation. Fundamentally, God built into man's conscience the things he more sharply focused in the Commandments. C. S. Lewis, in *The Abolition of Man*, says that if you check a number of ancient societies and cultures, you'll find surprising agreement in their ethical and moral standards, despite the widely divergent cultures. In effect he says: Man has a basic understanding of these standards that God, in creation, intends for all people.

Look at what the prophets had to say about the Ten Commandments. All along they told the people: "Get your act together and do what the Commandments say." But they predicted not only that the covenant people of Israel would adhere to these Commandments, but that one day God would write his laws in their hearts. This meant they would desire to fulfill his Commandments. And the prophets said these people would come from all nations—not just the small group of

Israelites, but all the nations of the world! God's commandments are principles designed for our well-being on both individual and societal levels. If that is true, failure to adhere to these commandments has results of the utmost seriousness for both believer and unbeliever.

# A Bridle, a Thermometer, a Mirror, a Guardian

Christians frequently talk as if they really know the Commandments, but how many could write them down without pulling out their Bibles first? How many people outside the church who say they live by these laws could list them?

You may ask, "What do we do with the Ten Commandments?" First, we need to use them as a compass, to give us our bearings. Many directionless people would have their lives dramatically transformed if they took the Commandments seriously.

Recently I talked to a troubled young man. He came to me in very difficult economic circumstances, with his life in a severe mess. "I've had the strangest thoughts going through my mind," he told me. "I'm getting desperate financially. I wouldn't want to tell you the things I've thought."

"Like issuing worthless checks?" I asked, as an insight came to me.

"Yes, how did you know?"

"I used to be a bank examiner," I said gently. "Have you thought of holding up a bank?" He told me he had. "Is that why you're here?" He told me it was.

"I'm frightened of the voices in my head—I'm frightened of the desperation in my heart. But," he shared, "one thing holds me fast: I know it is fundamentally wrong, because the Bible says, 'Thou shalt not steal.'"

In this young man's life the Commandments acted as a bridle to restrain him. It can work that way—even for those who do not always agree with these basic rules intellectually.

The Commandments may also act as a thermometer of our love for God. Do we have no other gods before him? Do we have no idols that we worship in his place? Do we tolerate abuse of God's name? These laws evaluate our behavior to show how we love him.

The Commandments also act as a mirror, showing us reality. As we look into the mirror of the Word of God, what do we discover? The truth the Bible describes in the words "By the law is the knowledge of sin" jumps right out at us. Gazing into that mirror, we see our flaws—and those of the world around us. When society tells us we may do as we please as long as we don't step on someone else's toes, it often tells us to do what God describes as categorically wrong. No matter how hard society tries to deny it, society is wrong, not God! When we look in the mirror, we see the reality of sin.

Finally the Ten Commandments can act as a guardian to bring us to Christ. Paul uses that expression. It means that the Commandments can take us only so far. They bring us to the point of realizing our own weakness and failure and sinfulness. Then they can introduce us to Christ, who alone can bring us forgiveness and the power to live differently. Someone has said the Commandments are the mirror, but not the soap. It shows me the reality of myself, but only the cleansing blood of Christ, his death on my behalf, can cleanse what the mirror shows is wrong.

We and our society need to ask the question, "Who needs the Ten Commandments?" And we both need the answer, which is simply, "We all do." Then we need to be able to explain why.

# ONE

You shall have
no other gods
before me.

Exodus 20:3

# 1
# Who Is Number One?

When the children of Israel had been in the wilderness only about three months, God called Moses to the side and reminded him that he had made a covenant with the people of Israel and had given them instructions about how they were to live. He had said he expected two basic things of his people: First, they were to love the Lord their God with all their heart and all their mind and all their strength; second, they were to love their neighbor as themselves.

Like the people of Israel of old, we need a little more detail about how we can do this, and God has answered us with his Ten Words. What does it mean to love God with all our hearts? In the first commandment we learn it means we must have him as the Supreme One in our lives. How can we live rightly in a covenant relationship with him? We need to have everything in subjection to him. Loving him with all our hearts and all our souls and all our strength means making a conscious decision to acknowledge him as the governing factor in our lives. Loving God means that having made him number one in our lives, we constantly reaffirm that decision, checking to see if he still is the dominant factor there. To do that we have to be aware of the competition for his place, understand the nature of God, and make a choice.

# What's the Competition?

"When you get into Canaan," God told the people of Israel, "you'll find competition—you'll find other gods that try to take my place. When you confront them, they must not be before me [or some translations say 'beside me']."

God wanted to prepare the Israelites for the different cultures and religious structures they'd find in Canaan, and he warned them to live among the Canaanites as the unique people of God. No other gods or cultural structures should take his place. "They are not to become more important than me; you are not to obey them rather than me," read his message.

What about those other gods? How did they come into being? To understand that, first we have to recognize man's inborn religious instinct. Edmund Burke said, "Man is by his constitution a religious animal." Calvin approvingly quoted Cicero when he said, "There is a seed of religion planted in all men." Wherever you come across people, they never seem to feel they are the beginning and the end. No matter how well we hide this instinct, if we're honest, we'll admit we need something bigger, something other, something grander. We want something that will be beneficial to us, something that will intervene on our behalf, something to take care of us, something to look up to.

In Romans 1:18-20, the apostle Paul makes clear God's work in all this:

> The wrath of God is being revealed from heaven against all the godlessness and wickedness of men who suppress

the truth by their wickedness, since what may be known about God is plain to them, because God has made it plain to them. For since the creation of the world God's invisible qualities—his eternal power and divine nature—have been clearly seen, being understood from what has been made, so that men are without excuse.

Paul says every person on the face of the earth has at least *some* knowledge of a great power, because God makes invisible things of his Spirit plain in the order of creation. Psalm 19 says something similar. David says, "The heavens declare the glory of God," and I imagine when he wrote that he thought of those long, quiet nights he spent looking after his sheep and staring up into the sky, overwhelmed by its awesomeness and confronted by the majesty of creation. In creation he saw a picture—a demonstration—of the glory of God.

None of this implies that everybody naturally has the same understanding of the reality of God or knowledge of him, but it does confirm that humans have a religious bent. How then have we arrived at so many different conclusions, when we started off with the same instincts?

Paul tells us people have suppressed the knowledge God gave in creation. Humankind intends to go away from what God has revealed and resents the little it knows of God by instinct. The apostle describes these attitudes as the essence of man's wickedness.

We were created in the image of God, yet we have fallen. Because we have departed from a relationship with him, all kinds of perversions have come into our lives, and humankind's undeniable ingenuity has become perverted ingenuity. Along with everything else, our religious instinct became perverted, and that has caused the many answers people provide—most of which are wrong.

When the Israelites went into Canaan, they confronted this perversion in the form of paganism. Along with primitive peoples everywhere, the Canaanites greatly depended on natural forces. In such societies everyone keenly understands that you have to sow the seed at the right time, that the temperature has to be right, that rain needs to come at the proper time, and that soil must be fertile in order to result in a good harvest. Such people recognize what we in our modern technological society forget: We cannot survive in our world without these powerful natural forces.

The primitive people of Canaan tried to identify these natural forces and decided they had the power of deities. When the primitive Canaanites heard the thunder rumble, they called it the deity of thunder. When they saw the sun shine, they saw a god behind the sun. They recognized gods of fertility and fecundity. Soon they ended up with thousands of gods, all clamoring for attention. Using their perverted religious instinct, they had put together two and two and come up with five—a pantheon of deities that formed the basis of their paganism.

The Canaanites believed that the gods of fertility and gods of the crops had to be appeased and placated, and there was a clear link, in their thinking, between the fertility of the soil and the fertility of their wives. In other words, crops and sex became almost synonymous. The worship of the gods of fertility became a worship of sexuality. In their perverted ingenuity, they produced all kinds of wonderfully perverted sexual activities in the name of religion. As a result, John Bright, a respected and renowned Old Testament scholar, says, "Canaanite religion presents us with no pretty picture. It was an extraordinarily debasing form of paganism."

What does this have to do with us? A lot. We also live in a very sophisticated pagan culture. Like the Israelites, we are called to be the people of God in the midst of a culture that does not honor him. Living in our sophisticated, rational, skilled, technological society, we too forget the Lord. We find it so easy to develop a nominal attachment to him, pushing him more and more into the background as we follow the gods of society. It doesn't take long before he no longer holds the number-one spot.

# What Is God Like?

In order to combat this tendency within us, God told us about himself in his laws. He didn't give the Ten Suggestions; instead he made some powerful statements in the Ten Commandments. Without introducing them in any ostentatious way, God simply comes right out and says, "Hey, folks, this is how it is. I want you to know these things."

## The unique God

In the first commandment, which forms the basis of the Ten Commandments, God reveals himself to us. He tells us he will not accept anything less than first place in our hearts. As follow-up he gave the revelation of Deuteronomy 6:4-5: "Hear, O Israel: The LORD our God, the LORD is one. Love the LORD your God with all your heart and with all your soul and with all your strength."

"The Lord is one." How sharply that description of God's nature stands out from the religious structures of the Canaanites, who based their gods on their own rationalization! The Canaanites looked at the great forces of nature, identifying them as deities, and named them. Then they tried to figure out how this pantheon of gods related to one another. They quickly built a religion based on human ingenuity.

7

In contrast, God starts with himself, revealing himself. "You don't have to figure out the deities, because I, the Deity, will reveal myself to you. The Lord your God, the Lord is one."

This holds two key points. First, God says he is the one and only, the absolutely unique one. To the Israelites in the wilderness that made a lot of sense. While they lived under the Egyptians, they had a terrible time, but God promised to bring them out. Before he did, there had been a big contest between the Lord and the gods of the Egyptians. In a nose-to-nose confrontation God had easily overcome the Egyptian gods. So when God said he was the one and only, the Israelites knew he was greater than all other gods; they'd seen proof of it themselves.

Second, when God claimed to be *one*, it meant there was unity in his person. Other gods always contradicted one another. Suppose the pagans had trouble with thunder—all kinds of storms rocked the earth—and the thunder god seemed really upset. So they gave him part of their sacrifice. But the thunder god got upset at the time they needed to give the goddess of grain and fertility attention. If they sacrificed to the god of thunder, she might get upset, and then what on earth would happen when they sowed the seed? They felt torn. How could they keep all their balls in the air, juggling to keep all the gods and goddesses happy?

The Lord said to the Israelites, "Hey, that will never happen with me. I'm *one*. I don't contradict myself; I don't fight against myself."

## God is God

In addition to telling the people he is one, God says he is God. That means he speaks with authority. All his actions

8

clearly demonstrate his unequivocal supremacy. To the Israelites he had already shown it in all he had done for them.

## God is gracious

Finally God wants his people to remember that he is gracious. At the beginning of the Ten Commandments he reminded them, "I am the Lord your God, who brought you out of Egypt, out of the land of slavery." He had shown his grace. He took a weak, helpless crowd of slaves—demoralized, disorganized, and oppressed by their captors—and intervened in their behalf. God brought them out of bondage and gave them a land they could never have claimed under other circumstances.

God reminded the Israelites of his graciousness in comparison to the other gods, whom they would have to appease. "Look what I have given you!" he declared.

Living in our society, where all kinds of gods, all kinds of ideas, and all kinds of philosophies abound, we desperately need the unique, powerful, and gracious Lord. We feel tempted to follow other gods and concepts, to explore them, and even to be caught up in worshiping them. Remember, we don't worship a God who brought us out of slavery, but one who intervened on our behalf through his death on a cross, saving us from death and hell. Our God has not simply brought us into a land of milk and honey; he gives us the greatest gift of eternal life through his Son, our Lord Jesus. Our God has not filled the Nile with blood and frogs and all other kinds of nasty creepy-crawlies, but he has raised Jesus from the dead. Ours is the God of revelation, who commands: "Don't insult me by bringing all the other gods alongside me, and don't dare insult me by putting them ahead of me. Why? Because I am the Lord your God who brought you out of Egypt, the place of slavery, out of the bondage of sin, and I, the Lord, am one."

# Opposition to the Commandment

God makes this powerful commandment: "You shall have no other gods before me," yet we tend to ask, "Why not, Lord?" If we look at the Israelites' story, we can immediately see what happens if we oppose God's very nature. How quickly we fall into syncretism or sensualism!

## Syncretism

*Syncretism* means pulling a lot of divergent things together to try to make a whole out of them. The children of Israel faced such a religious situation in Canaan. When they came into a town, the little king of that town would have his own special gods, the local deities. When the Israelites captured the town and overthrew the king, they were tempted to gather up the gods and keep them to themselves. Then they'd have Jehovah *and* the gods of the town. They'd go into the next town—little king, little pile of gods different from all the others—conquer it, and keep those gods as well. In no time at all the people of Israel, who theoretically had Jehovah as their God also had collected a whole pantheon of gods on their travels. The first commandment gets lost in the crowd.

For the same reason God warned his people not to intermarry with the Canaanites. If you married a Canaanite girl, it wasn't just "marry me, marry my family." She brought along her own gods, so it meant "marry me, marry my family, marry my gods." In a short time the Israelites ended up with the most unholy, syncretic mishmash of religion imaginable.

God warned them that if they did this, forgetting the God who brought them out of Egypt, they would become utterly confused.

With our 20/20 hindsight we recognize the failings and sins of the Israelites. But what about us? We profess to honor the Lord, but our society doesn't. We listen to our society, observe it, compete in it. Whether or not we like it, we're part of it. If we want to get along in it, we think we have to listen to it, agree with it, appease it. Soon what happens? We diminish the uniqueness of the Lord. He no longer holds first place, and we end up with a syncretic Christianity.

In our syncretism, we have the audacity to want to bring in the things that are so bad that he died for them; we want the freedom to have them coexist with the Christ who died for them. The word comes down through the centuries: "Thou shalt have no other gods before me—thou shalt have no other gods beside me." Why? Because Jesus is the Risen Lord. He's Number One.

## Sensualism

The paganism of the Canaanites demonstrated sensuality. Human beings have a God-given sensuality, but like everything else, it's been perverted. All the senses our Lord gave us he intended us to employ in understanding and appreciating him. But we have used them wrongly in many ways. Sometimes we allow our senses to so dominate us that we push aside the truth, becoming purely sensual people.

God knew that if the Israelites, who were a very sensual people, got into an area filled with seductively sensual paganism, they would face some real danger. Surrounded by attractive sensuality that pandered to their inner, undisciplined desires, whims, and caprices, if they didn't keep on track, they would go off after other gods and would move into other areas, wandering away from the One True God.

That's the problem in our society today. Our twentieth-century technological, sophisticated paganism also caters to our inner, ill-disciplined sensuality. We find it all so attractive and utterly seductive. If we don't keep in mind that the Lord our God is one, that he has dealt graciously with us and brought us out of the house of bondage and made a covenant of grace with us, we'll end up miles from God, wrapped up in syncretism and all other kinds of things that are anathema to him, and we'll be a religious mess! We have to honor Number One.

## What's the Choice?

How do we avoid wandering away from the God who is one? First we need to make a choice. At the end of Joshua's life, the leader of the Israelites reminded the people of their covenant with God: "Now fear the LORD and serve him with all faithfulness. Throw away the gods your forefathers worshiped beyond the River and in Egypt, and serve the LORD. But if serving the LORD seems undesirable to you, then choose for yourselves this day whom you will serve, whether the gods your forefathers served beyond the River, or the gods of the Amorites, in whose land you are living. But as for me and my household, we will serve the LORD" (Josh. 24:14-15).

To these people who had seen the goodness, power, and grace of God, Joshua put forth a challenge. "You are living in flat contravention of what God has said. It's time to shape up! Choose this day which way you want to go."

Elijah had a similar confrontation. He lived in the time of King Ahab, who had married Jezebel, a woman from Tyre. When she came to Ahab, the queen brought her gods with her. So the nation worshiped both the Tyrian gods and Jehovah—a terrible mess. Conflict arose, and in the end, Elijah stood on Mount Carmel and said to the people, "If Jehovah is God, follow him. If he isn't, forget it. If the baals are the gods, follow them." He also came up with this great statement: "How long will you waver between two opinions?" (1 Kings 18:21).

"You can't have your cake and eat it, too," he says in effect.

Jesus said, "You can't worship God and Money. You've got to decide whether or not he is Lord."

Today we face the same decision. Is God God? Is Christ Lord? If you want to acknowledge God and Christ, will you follow through on the implications of that decision? What God requires is unadulterated allegiance, that you should respond in love to him because of his great love for you. Since he gave himself for you, God deserves your unreserved gift of yourself to him. Christ the Lord demands first place in your affections, that he should be the authoritative figure in your life—the one, the only, the true God. The choice is yours.

Some people have never really faced up to the absolute necessity for a basic, initial choice. "How long will you waver between two opinions?" God asks. How long will you feel you have enough of God to keep you religious, but not enough to change you? How long will you feel Christ will be satisfied with your honoring him enough so you don't go to hell, but not honoring him enough so you can live as if you love him? How long will you say, "Christ is Lord," yet make

13

it obvious that 1,001 things rate ahead of him? "Choose," he demands.

## Evaluate the Choice

Once we make that initial choice, we continually need to evaluate it. In the same way the gods of the Cannanites seduced the Israelites, the gods of our society, our cultural norms, can seduce us from the love of God.

At the end of each day, ask yourself: Was Jesus Christ my Lord today? Did I serve him faithfully today? Did I love him deeply? Did I worship him exclusively? Did I find all the other little gods in my life making unwarranted incursions into my faith? Did I live a double standard, a double life? What will you discover? If you're honest, honoring the Lord will require a constant, disciplined walk of obedience and dependence, including repentance, restoration, and renewal.

Today I need to decide: "Whom will I serve; who will be the Lord of my life?"

1. What are the two basic things God expects of his people? How do the Ten Commandments relate to those over-arching directions?

2. What other "gods" vied for God's place in the hearts of the Israelites? What "gods" plague Christians today?

3. Why did God's revelation of himself to the people of Israel emphasize that he is "one God"?

4. What proofs had the Israelites seen that God's authority was supreme? What proofs have you seen in your own experience?

5. The Israelites had also experienced God's graciousness. What undeserved gifts or treatment have you received from our gracious God?

6. Define *syncretism* and *sensualism*. How do they affect your view of God?

# TWO

You shall not make for yourself
an idol in the form
of anything in heaven above
or on the earth beneath or in the
waters below. You shall not
bow down to them
or worship them;
for I, the LORD your God,
am a jealous God,
punishing the children
for the sin of the fathers
to the third and fourth generation
of those who hate me,
but showing love
to a thousand generations
of those who love me
and keep my commandments.

Exodus 20:4-6

# 2
# Making God in Our Image

Thomas Watson, the Puritan preacher, said in the seventeenth century, "In the first commandment worshiping a false God is forbidden. In this, however, the second commandment, worshiping the true God in a false manner is forbidden." His few words described the essence of idolatry.

When a pastor preaches on idolatry, it can be one of the easiest things he does, or the hardest. If he takes the easy road, he lists his prejudices and the faults of his congregation and then really lays it on them. The hard way is to find the underlying concern in Scripture regarding idolatry and to preach about that.

I want to deal with this commandment in the hard way, to give you a general application of Scripture that will allow the Holy Spirit to speak to your heart about idolatry.

## God Denounces Idolatry

In the second commandment God clearly denounces idolatry so we cannot mistake his reaction to it. He provides his people with some clear and specific guidelines.

## Don't make idols

Notice first of all that the second commandment bans the making of idols. He says to his people, "You shall not make yourself an idol in the form of anything above the earth, on the earth or beneath the waters." Some people call this "classical three-tier Hebrew cosmology," which simply means that the Hebrews thought the universe had three levels: the heavens, the earth, and the waters beneath the earth. Others apply this more specifically, saying that when you talk about creatures above the earth, it means spiritual forces; creatures on the earth means material things; what is under the earth means the denizens of death and the strange life hereafter.

No matter how you represent this description, it all comes down to one thing: In every single area of the universe, you can't use anything else to represent the Creator. No material, spiritual, or strange, esoteric monster can take the place of God in your life. Never represent the Creator by anything created. That's the fundamental rule.

## Don't worship idols

Second, God says, "Not only should you not make idols, you shall not bow down to them or worship them." It's one thing to make an idol and another to worship it. In the strictest sense of the term, I suppose I have some idols in my study at home.

On one occasion when I visited India, a pastor friend of mine and I got into his car. I had to move a little sack in order to sit down. When I picked it up, it clanked, and I asked, "What do you have there?"

"I'm just going to trash those things," my friend replied.

"What are they?"

He pulled one out, and I saw a beautiful piece of Indian copper work. "You're going to trash that?" I asked.

"Yes, it's a Hindu idol. The family it belonged to has just become Christians, and they have been baptized, and I'm taking their idols away. They have given them up, and I'm going to destroy them."

"I'd like to take one of them home," I told him. My friend found it hard to understand why. "It is a beautiful piece of copper work, as far as I'm concerned," I said. "It would become an idol only if I bowed down and worshiped it." He gave it to me only reluctantly, with the provision that every time I saw it I would remember to pray for Hindus lost in pagan darkness.

God says, on the one hand, do not represent the Creator by anything created, but also do not render to anything that which rightly and exclusively belongs to God. Do not give away the worship, the adoration, and the devotion that are exclusively the right of God himself.

That may seem strange to say to a sophisticated twentieth-century audience, but we, too, have our idols. Herbert Schlossberg said in his book *Idols for Destruction:* "Anyone with a hierarchy of values has placed something at its apex, and whatever that is is the God he serves." Everyone has a hierarchy of values. We say some things are good and some are bad. We say some things are better and some are worse.

How do you distinguish good from bad? How do you measure better and worse? Somewhere along the line you have established a standard of evaluation—you have the apex of your hierarchy, the thing that's most important. That, says Schlossberg, is the god you serve.

We constantly need to evaluate what forms the apex of our hierarchy. If we have rendered to it that which is exclusively God's, we have become idolatrous.

## Don't miscalculate God's reaction

In his denunciation of idolatry, God says, "Don't miscalculate my reaction to it." Exodus 20:5 says, "I, the LORD your God, am a jealous God." We don't like to think of that aspect of God, and many people read this far and no farther. But we need to remember that when we take all the attributes of God together, none of them are mutually incompatible. The holiness of God and the jealousy of God work together, so he exhibits a holy jealousy and a jealous holiness.

Perhaps we can understand more easily if we identify jealousy as "a zealousness for what is right—an utter, total, burning, consuming commitment to hold on to that which is right." In this sense God is jealous. With all the intensity and integrity of his being, God will defend and insist on his rightful place at the center of the universe, on the throne of his creatures' hearts. He will resist with his almighty power anything that infringes on his position.

Even more than we dislike the idea of God's jealousy, we avoid the idea that he punishes the children for the sins of the fathers, down to the third and fourth generations. Many people read that and respond, "If that's your God, you're welcome to him. I'll have a different one, thank you." But think for a moment: if you go to a psychologist, chances are you'll engage in psychotherapy that will identify your emotional aberration by looking into your past. The therapist may ask questions about your parents and grandparents. That psychologist affirms the truth of the nature of God, because to a great extent you've become what you are because of your parents' and grandparents' influence.

In effect God says, "If I do not have my rightful place in people's lives, if other things take my place, the ramifications and repercussions pass inevitably from generation to generation." Again he denounces idolatry.

## Don't forget God's grace

In addition God says, "Don't forget my grace!" In marked contrast to the statement about punishing the children he goes on to say, "I show love." The Hebrew word here is *hesed*, meaning "love, mercy, grace, kindness"; it's an all-encompassing, beautiful covenant word of the Old Testament. He shows this love, kindness, mercy, and grace to thousands. The structure of the Hebrew here contrasts three or four generations with thousands of generations. Remember, when God speaks firmly, he also remains ready to act graciously, and his grace is always infinitely greater than his judgment. Paul puts it this way, "Where sin [and accordingly judgment] increased, grace increased all the more" (Rom. 5:20).

## Be on your guard!

Not only did God address the issue of idolatry in the Commandments, he also mentions it throughout Scripture. The prophets have a number of trenchant words about idolatry. Remember, God warned the children of Israel, coming into the Promised Land, to avoid the gods of the Cannanites. If you look at the ministry of the prophets, you'll realize the children of Israel ignored God's warning. As Jeremiah 10:2-5 says:

Do not learn the ways of the nations or be terrified by signs in the sky, though the nations are terrified by them. For the customs of the peoples are worthless; they cut a tree out of the forest, and a craftsman shapes it with his chisel. They adorn it with silver and gold; they fasten it with hammer and nails so it will not totter. Like a scarecrow in a melon patch, their idols cannot speak; they must be carried because they cannot walk. Do not fear them; they can do no harm nor can they do any good.

The books of the other prophets hold many similar passages, reminding God's people of the powerlessness of the idols God denounces. Yet the Israelites had an amazing propensity to slip into worshiping the powerlessness and to abandon themselves to what was worthless and meaningless. Their prophets warned them to avoid it like the plague.

In the New Testament Jesus doesn't say much about idolatry, except for his statement, "No one can serve two masters. Either he will hate the one and love the other, or he will be devoted to the one and despise the other. You cannot serve both God and Money" (Matt. 6:24). He said little about idolatry because the people he ministered to didn't have a problem with that.

But when Paul moved out into the Gentile world, he found all kinds of idolatry. He faced it with the Corinthians, who offered meat to idols. The pagan people would offer their meat offering to idols—prime rib, corn-fed, the best beef— nothing but first class for the idols. But the idols had little appetites and the priests had big appetites, so the priests left a little for the idols and took most for themselves. They still had far more than they could handle, so they took some down to the butchers. The butchers sold it to the restaurants, so if you wanted a good meal and took your friends to the best restaurant in Corinth, when you ordered prime rib, you got meat offered to idols.

The Christians said, "We can't go to restaurants. We can't order the best cuts of meat, because this is all involved in idolatry." They saw it as a big issue.

What did Paul say? The apostle told them, "The idols are nothing in themselves, but demonic powers lie behind them. Be on your guard about idolatry because of those powers behind the idols, which will sidetrack you from God. Stay on your toes, because you could innocently get yourself into trouble this way" (see 1 Cor. 8). But in Colossians and Ephesians, he says that "greed or covetousness is idolatry" (Eph. 5:3; Col. 3:5). Why? Because greed and covetousness mean I've given myself in utter devotion to the created *thing* rather than to the Creator.

## The Dangers of Idolatry

"Hey, what's the big deal about all this?" you may ask. Maybe you still feel like the little boy who had supper with his parents one night and let slip a little word he'd learned in school that day. He wanted to practice it. Dad, who heard that word often in the office, didn't even notice, but his mother acted horror-struck, banished him from the table, and told him to stay in his room all night.

After the boy had gone to his room, a terrible thunderstorm blew in. The lightning flashed and thunder crashed; the rain came splashing down, and the mother's heart went pitter-pat as she wondered how her child was. She crept up to his bedroom and quietly opened the door. There she saw her small boy, silhouetted against the window, and heard him say, "God, all this for one little word?"

Do you feel as if God has become somewhat over-reactionary to idolatry? God's response shows us how dangerous idolatry can be. Idolatry may affect your spiritual life in seven ways.

## Turning means into ends

If all people have some instinctive knowledge of God's existence, they want to respond to him. But when they look for ways to do that and turn to their culture and the things they make and begin to use their ingenuity to produce things to help them understand the invisible, they enter into idolatry. As they use tangible things to reach out to the intangible, the things take the place of the intangible, and the means become ends in themselves. They do exactly what God says not to do: The created takes the place of the Creator.

That may sound strictly pagan, but Christians do this, too. Have you ever noticed that, though we use many methods to worship God, sometimes they become so important to us that we lose all sight of the God we worship, and the forms become an end in themselves? For example, at one time most people couldn't read, so the church developed a liturgy to help everyone memorize Scriptures. That was very helpful. But when, as often happens, the liturgy became worshiped instead of God, it lost its helpfulness.

I don't mean that as a shot at liturgy—every church has some form of liturgy—but it shows how, in the life of the Christian, the created may begin to take the place of the Creator.

## Substituting things for people

Next, idolatry makes *things* more important than people. God has not revealed himself as a power, or an entity, or a thing, but as a *person* with whom we can relate. We share a friendship in which we know him, love him, and respond in gratitude to him. But the idolater makes a mistake in substituting things for him. Initially he may even put good things in God's place, but by his doing that, those things become bad. Even a ministry may begin to replace the Lord in importance—I know, because I've done it!

At one stage in my career it looked as if my preaching days were over. Although I had been at it for many years, tremendous new opportunities had begun to open before me. I stood right on the edge when I suffered an illness that threatened to stop it all. For the only time I can remember I suffered depression. I did not feel at all happy with the situation. My concern, I told myself, stemmed from the fact that I loved to preach about the Lord Jesus. Then in my own heart God spoke to me powerfully, saying, "Stuart Briscoe, do you love preaching about the Lord Jesus more than you love the Lord Jesus about whom you preach?" The answer was yes. I knew I felt upset with the Lord Jesus because I could not preach about him. If I had been excited about *him*, it would not have mattered whether or not I could have preached about him. I felt as if the Spirit of God said, "You get things in perspective, and you will preach again. Until you get it in perspective, you'll never preach."

When a good thing becomes overly important to us, it becomes our possession. We get so excited about it that we worship ourselves rather than the Lord, as in the case of my ministry, which had turned into idolatry. That sin destroyed the ministry's effectiveness.

## Placing imagination above revelation

In addition, idolatry places people's imagination above God's revelation. Look at some of the representations of the gods made by various cultures, and their creators' imagination will amaze you. Some Egyptian gods have the figure of a human being with the head of a crocodile, or ox, or lion. When those sculptors thought of a sudden and fierce god, nothing seemed more sudden and fierce in anger than a crocodile. Nothing seemed more brave and courageous than a lion—and so on. So they used their imagination to create fantastic gods that represented these concepts.

Surely God has given us imagination, but our imagination, too, is fallen. It's not pure and clean, but easily becomes warped and twisted by our thinking, which does not follow God's truth, but our own fantasies. As J. I. Packer has said, "Metal images are the consequence of mental images." Instead of accepting himself as a person made in God's image, the idolater tries to remake God in his own image, to bring God down to a "comfortable" size.

When we do this, our imagination begins to destroy our lives as we turn from his truth to our fantasy, for we find ourselves estranged from the real world, divorced from truth.

As Christians, we may do this by trying to turn God into some kind of celestial Santa Claus. We don't like the sometimes wrathful God of Scripture and much prefer the one in our fantasy world. In making ourselves comfortable, we totally destroy reality as far as the holy God is concerned. We have put in God's place that which we manufactured ourselves.

## Limiting God's transcendence

Idolatry also imposes limits on divine transcendence. When Solomon created the temple, he felt awestruck by the magnificent building until God deigned to enter it. Then he lost interest in physical surroundings. He worshiped the Lord, declaring, "God, even the heaven of heavens cannot contain you. Will you deign to live in a place made by human hands?" (see 1 Kings 8:27). He had the right idea.

The idolater thinks, This thing I have created contains God. This thing I devote myself to, this thing for which I live, this thing for which I will give myself—this is God. What happens? The great, transcendent God becomes squished down into a totally insulting situation.

We Christians cut God down to our own size, destroying reverence. For example, have you ever seen a parent collect the kids from the church nursery and take them to the sanctuary? The kids start running around, jumping and dancing, parading up and down the steps. Mother comes rushing up, saying, "Don't do that! This is God's house."

The kids start looking around. "Where is God? Is he in the booth back there? Is he in that box?"

Are they really in God's house? No. But some people would like the church to be God's house, because then they could keep him in there, visit him once a week, like a sick relative, and run their lives the way they want to. They've brought God down to their own size.

## Putting humans in control

Idolatry places ourselves in control of God, but at a terrible price. Isaiah describes what had happened to his people this way, "Your idols have become a burden to you." His words reminded the Hebrews of the actions of the Babylonians—a pagan people who had conquered them and taken them into captivity. Wherever they went, the Babylonians carried their idols with them. Isaiah 46 compares the idolatry of the Hebrews to that when it says, "Listen, your idols are a burden to you, because you carry them," but it goes on to remind them, "But when God brought your forefathers out of Egypt, he carried them" (see Isa. 46:1-4).

Who carries whom means a lot. If I worship idols, I carry them; I control my god. Because I've made him small, I can put him where I want. He won't intrude on my life.

But look at the repercussions of that in my life. If people control God, it means we are gods. If I'm god, then God help us. Like the self-made person, who deifies himself, I will worship my creator—myself. Like the self-made man, I will get terribly upset when others don't come and worship at my church, the "First Church of Stuart Briscoe." Every day I will invite others to idolatry and become terribly upset when they don't share my vision of myself. If, as such a church implies, people are the beginning and the end, we are of all creatures most miserable.

## Fashioning God in a popular style

Idolatry fashions God in the popular style, making him suit the world around us. See how it happened with the children of Israel. While all the nations around them developed polytheism, they stood out because they believed in one God, who had revealed himself to them.

When he made the covenant with them, God warned his people against syncretism, but they didn't listen. In the end they became confused. They lost sight of their unique covenant relationship with God. Finally they so degenerated that they even threw their children into the fiery furnaces of the pagan god Moloch. The Israelites remade God in the contemporary style.

When we do this in our lives, we totally destroy our distinctiveness as the people of God. How can we be distinguished from the antichrist, anti-God society surrounding us?

The Christian church always faces the tension of holding to the eternal revelation yet communicating it to today's world. Some of us easily remain relevant but lose faithfulness. Others may stay faithful and lose relevance. We all need to ask: How can I be faithful to the Word of God and relevant to a society that does not know him—or even want to know him?

Each of us faces this tension not to get so caught up in our culture that we lose sight of the Lord. If we do so, we finish up as strangers to Scripture, unknown in the courts of heaven.

## Detracting from God's image

Finally, idolatry detracts from God's chosen image. If we remake God in our image, we have forgotten that God made people in his image, that the image was marred, and that he sent Christ, the express image of his person. If I make up my own images, I ignore Christ. I will not understand the unique place God gave man, and my idolatry will denigrate my understanding of man and will depreciate my experience and appreciation of Christ.

All our idolatry attempts to whittle God down, suit him to our way of doing things, fit him in a "comfortable" pattern that does not harm our own ideas or challenge our way of thinking. By the time we have finished, we have denied God his power, muddied or defaced his image, and left ourselves with pitiful, empty lives that benefit neither him nor us.

Idolatry is serious business. God cannot ignore it. We do so at our peril!

1. God commands us not to make or worship idols. Compare the pagan's handmade "gods" to our "gods"—things that have become more important to us than God. Is God Number One in your life?

2. How does our idolatry affect the generations to come? How can God's grace affect them?

3. Sometimes we let *things*—even good things—become more important than God. How can you be sure to worship God himself?

4. How can your imagination get in the way of true worship?

5. How can Christians live in today's society, yet worship God without falling into idolatry?

# THREE

You shall not misuse
the name of the LORD your God,
for the LORD will not
hold anyone guiltless
who misuses his name.

Exodus 20:7

# 3
# Using God for My Own Ends

Most of us are familiar with the text of the third commandment in the King James Version translation: "Thou shalt not take the name of the Lord thy God in vain." Chances are that we have used the expression "taking the name of the Lord in vain." But what do we mean when we say it?

Most regular churchgoers would probably tell us the commandment has something to do with bad language, with cursing and swearing and profanity. When you start to talk about it, most of them will relax, knowing they don't do anything like that—at least not often.

In saying that, though, they have missed something important. There's much more in the idea of this commandment than we've commonly allowed for.

## What's in a Name?

What's in a name? I want to try to answer that question with particular reference to "the name of the Lord," which we have been warned not to take in vain. What does a name mean, and how can we misuse it?

## Reputation

Generally, a name speaks of the reputation of the person who bears it. In the Bible we see several examples of different reputations based on names. In Genesis 11, the story of the tower of Babel, we learn that the people had come together in a large city with the objective of making a name for themselves. They planned to build a tower that would reach up into the heavens; they wanted to look good for their own gain. In effect they said, "We don't really need God; we can handle this life ourselves, and we will establish our own reputation, apart from God."

But is it always wrong to make a name for yourself? The Proverbs say a good name is more to be desired than riches, meaning that a good reputation, in the long run, has a lot more value than money. Many people have made lots of money and ruined their reputations doing it. Others have impeccable reputations, but have never translated that into funds. The verse says: "If you've got to choose, always choose the good name, the good reputation." The writer didn't encourage anyone to look good for his own gain and instructed his readers not to put money before honor.

Philippians 2 tells us that God gave the Lord Jesus a name that is above every name, that at the name of Jesus every knee shall bow and every tongue confess that he is Lord. Those words speak of Christ's powerful reputation.

The people we find in the Scriptures understood this concept of reputation. They named their children very carefully. They named a child for something that reflected the desires they had for him, or they gave him a name that related to his birth. In all cases they considered the meaning of the name a child would bear before they gave it to him.

My own name has something of a special significance in this same way. Just before I was born, my father picked up a book called *In the Heart of Savagedom*, the story of two single women who worked as missionaries in the Belgian Congo. These intrepid ladies took off into the wild jungle and got into all kinds of hair-raising escapades. It was a very exciting book, and my dad got inspired by these two women who took on the whole Belgian Congo.

He said to my mother, who at the time was not particularly interested in reading a book but was very interested in getting rid of the load that was me, "If this kid's a boy, we'll call him Stuart," because one of the missionaries was named Eva Stuart Watt. My father hoped something of this intrepid missionary would rub off on me. When I was small, my dad told me the story, and I've always kept it in mind.

Many years later I preached in Belfast, Northern Ireland; at the end of the service I stood at the rear of the church and shook hands with everyone as they left. At the end of the line came a tiny, wizened old lady, carrying an umbrella with which she reinforced her points—and she had a lot of points she wanted to make. She began to poke me with her umbrella as she said, "Our pastor's no good, no good. You come be our pastor."

"Well," I said, "I don't think he would like it if I just arrived and said, 'Okay, I'm going to be your pastor.' You can't do it that way."

"He's no good," she told me again. (She really wasn't too high on her pastor.) "They don't like me in this church, either. They just don't like me."

"Oh," I said, "I'm sure—"

"No," she told me emphatically, "they don't.. Don't say they do, when I tell you they don't."

"All right, why would they not like you?"

"It's the prostitutes I bring in," she replied forthrightly.

"You bring in prostitutes?"

"Yes, they're gorgeous, gorgeous prostitutes, and I bring them to church. They're beautiful girls. They've got terrible stories, and they need the Lord Jesus; but when I bring them into church, all those people move out. They don't want to sit next to them. I love these prostitutes."

I enjoyed this brave little old lady, who told me, "I think you would like them, too. If you would come and be our pastor, you'd be fine with our prostitutes." She did most of the talking, and we only began to end our conversation after the church had been empty about half an hour. As I left I asked her name. "I'm Eva Stuart Watt's sister," she told me. I felt excited to meet her and told her my story. After that it took me another half hour to convince her I wouldn't come be their pastor.

What's in a name? Reputation! In my family Eva Stuart Watt had one for her missionary zeal that could not be dimmed by circumstances. Her name said something about what you could expect from her.

## Character

A name could also be a prophetic statement in terms of a child's character. The Jews knew this. "Thou shalt call his name Jesus." Why? It was a common name, derived from Joshua. But Mary was instructed to "call his name Jesus" because it meant "Savior." The character of the Son of God was built into that name.

## Personality

A name may also speak of the personality involved. Sometimes personalities change, as we see in the story of Jacob.

Jacob wrestled with God—a silly thing to do. He wrestled all night, and in the end God let Jacob do what he wanted. God gives you a lot of room to wrestle with him, but in the end, he says, "I've just got to be getting on to someone who's going to be more responsive." So he clinked Jacob's thigh out of joint.

If you've taken part in the sport, you know that once your thigh goes out of joint, you rather lose interest in wrestling. So Jacob lay down and said, "Okay, I've been resisting you up until now; now I'll rely on you."

And God replied, "All right, that's fine. Your name was Jacob, but it will be Israel." The Lord had detected the change in this man. *Jacob* means "crook, slimy character." *Israel* means "prince of God." What's in a name? It describes what you're like.

## Authority

A name also carries a sense of authority. In the beginning God created the world. How did he do it? First he said, "Let there be light." By the very naming of it, light came into existence. God made everything out of nothing—even the names. But the names held a significance. In the giving of the name is authority.

God made Adam and told him, "All right, Adam, now there are lots of animals around here. It's your responsibility to name them." In this way God said, "I have authority over the whole of creation. I'll delegate a lot of it to man, and man will demonstrate that authority in the naming of these things."

## God's name

How do reputation, character, and authority relate to the name of the Lord? In the Old Testament God revealed himself by his name, in marked contrast to the false gods all around. The false gods, instead of informing men of their names, received names from their creators. As a human gave a god its name, he also gave it personality, character, and a reputation. It all resulted from human ingenuity, a person imposing his wishes on his gods.

## God is knowable

But when God revealed his name, he took the initiative, saying, "You can't make me the way you want me to be. *I am*. As the 'I am' I will demonstrate who I am, so that you will have no questions about it." God chose to let us know himself in his true nature.

When God introduced himself to Abraham or Moses or anyone else, in effect, he said, "I'm knowable. I want to introduce myself to you."

Americans are great at introducing themselves. When I first came to America, over twenty years ago, I remember going into the deep South. The very first time I preached, a great big man came up to me and said, "Hi, I'm Bill." At first I didn't understand what he'd said, but I got it interpreted that he was saying, "Hello, my name is Bill." Then he shook hands, grabbed me, and put his arm around me. Then at the end of the talk he gave me a big hug. Now the British are terribly proper, and nobody had ever done that to me, probably not even my father. Being so terribly proper, that sort of affection isn't common. This person who came and identified himself really took me aback, because he opened himself up to me so quickly. From that first meeting I learned a lot about Bill.

As soon as I introduce myself to somebody, I reveal my identity, saying, "Hey, folks, I am knowable." God did the same thing. When he named himself, he invited humankind to know him in a special way. Remember, when he revealed himself to the patriarchs, he really said, "This is who I am. Study my name. It will give you my reputation, my character, and a feel for my authority. These will give you an opportunity for intimacy with the living God."

Daniel says that they who know their God shall be strong and do exploits (Dan. 11:32, KJV). Why? Because they have an intimacy of relationship with God.

Remember the young David, chomping at the bit because his big brothers had gone off to war and he had to stay home? One day his mom said, "Okay, you can go to war. Take these supplies to your big brothers." So David went off, hating that bag of supplies, but glad he could go. When he got to the campsite of the army, he found his brothers and all the other big soldiers cowering in the bottom of a trench. Out on the hillside stood a big giant, saying, "Come on, your champion shall fight me. If I win, my side wins. If you win, your side wins" (see 1 Sam. 17).

What an excellent way of settling international differences. Of course, only the Philistines wanted to do it that way, because they had Goliath. The Israelites weren't in a hurry to answer that challenge. David, the teenager, asked his brothers, "Why don't you have a go at it?"

They answered, "Mind your own business."

"Why don't you go?" he asked again. Nobody was interested.

David asked so persistently that in the end word got to King Saul. King Saul stood head and shoulders over anyone else. Guess who *should* have gone out to Goliath? "No way!" said Saul. So in the end young David prevailed on King Saul to let him go.

I can't believe Saul let him go. But he did what adults do when teenagers embarrass them. Saul tried to put David in his own armor, lowered him inside, clamped it shut, and screwed down the helmet. Out of that tin can a little voice cried, "Let me out of here!"

David said, "I don't need all that stuff." He went to a brook and got five smooth stones, wound up his sling, and flexed his wrist, elbow, and shoulder. He sauntered up to Goliath, who just stood there with his spear like a weaver's beam. Goliath asked David, "Am I a dog? Am I a dog that you should come to me like that?"

David answered, "No, you're no dog. You're a very big giant. I've come to get you."

Goliath's deep voice rumbled, "You've come with your sword and spear?"

David calmly replied, "No, but I come to you in the name of the Lord."

What did David mean? He meant, "You can keep your swords, your spears. I come with the intimate knowledge of the living God." David knew the power of God; he relied on God's force, God's initiative, God's protection.

## God saves us

When we know God and his protection and when we live intimately with him, coming to terms with him as he is, we experience his salvation. David certainly did in his battle with Goliath. The apostle Paul, writing to the Corinthians, says that through faith in God's name we are saved. Does that mean we should use his name like *abracadabra*—"Jesus, Jesus, Jesus"—magic? No. In God's revelation, as we put our faith in him as he really is, the power of his salvation becomes released in our lives. When that happens, you have the opportunity to be identified with God through his name.

Saul of Tarsus traveled along the road to Damascus when suddenly a bright light smote him. In that light he saw the risen Christ, and suddenly Saul realized Christ was for real. He fell on his face, saying, "Lord, what would you have me do?" Now blind, he made his way into Damascus, waiting because the Lord needed someone to minister to him. No one felt terribly enthusiastic about ministering to Saul of Tarsus. He was a well-known persecutor of Christians. To minister to him was to sign your own death warrant.

But God found an obedient man called Ananias. "What are you doing, Ananias?"

"Just packing, Lord."

"Where are you going?"

"Getting out of here."

"Why, Ananias?"

"Because Saul of Tarsus is coming, Lord, and he's a nasty, nasty gentleman. He doesn't like followers of the Way. He doesn't like those who bear your name, Lord. He exterminates them one by one. I may be next."

"Well, before you run, Ananias, I have a little witnessing job for you."

"It won't take long, will it? To whom shall I go?"

"Saul of Tarsus."

Ananias went. He entered the room with great trepidation. To his intense delight, he saw that Saul was blind. The Lord said, "Lay your hands on him, Ananias."

Ananias laid his hand on Saul's head and started with two beautiful words, "Brother Saul, I've come to tell you that God has chosen you to bear his name. And I'm also here to tell you that you must suffer great things for his name."

What did Ananias mean? God has revealed his name, shown that he is knowable, invited us to intimacy, promised power and protection in the knowledge of his name, and given us the privilege of putting his name upon ourselves. As we do that we so identify with him that we bear the privilege of making the knowable God known. We bear his name, but not without cost.

Dave Ramsdale is a missionary pilot in South America. Together we got into a little float plane on an oxbow lake, which lies off one of the head waters of the Amazon River. As we took off over the impenetrable jungle, Dave told me we might visit one of the primitive Indian tribes he ministers to. He told me that on his last furlough he had flown professionally and had the ratings and skill to fly out of the busy New York City area airports.

Below us was a landscape that didn't look the least bit like New York City. Eventually we landed in a little jungle creek. While visiting the Indians, we covered our legs with sulfur to keep the mosquitoes from eating us alive.

Getting back into the plane, I asked Dave why he chooses to fly in the middle of nowhere. In effect Dave Ramsdale told me it's a privilege to bear the name of Jesus to people who have never heard it. Despite the hardships, he stays on for the privilege of bearing Christ's name.

## How Do We Take God's Name in Vain?

Even though we understand all this about God's name, how have we at times taken it in vain? How do we still misuse it? Remember the word *vanity* occurs quite a lot in the Old Testament. It means "to empty of content, to make irrelevant." How can I take the name of the Lord and empty it of content? When have I made it irrelevant? What have I done to take the name of the Lord and twist it into shapes he never intended it to go in? That's what this commandment is about.

44

Folks in the Old Testament understood the concept of using God's name in vain. Today before you can borrow money from someone, he'll check on your credit rating; he wants empirical evidence that you'll repay. The Israelites didn't have credit ratings. How did a man know if you'd repay his loan? The Israelites took oaths, calling on the name of the Lord. They'd say, "The Lord do so-and-so to me, also, unless . . ." That's where the phrase "as the Lord liveth" became so popular; the Israelites also used this expression to show their dependence on God to control the results of the promise.

What they originally meant was I'm making this promise knowing that the Lord God knows everything, including this promise. I'm taking this oath knowing that God is my judge. God knows I'm making this promise, and he will judge me if I don't keep it. That kind of oath had profound significance.

But people get casual. After a while the Israelites would call on the name of the Lord when they didn't mean it. They would say, "As the Lord liveth," but they were just empty words. Although they spoke God's name, they didn't think of his oversight. When they used his name in their oaths, they no longer considered their accountability to him. They emptied God's name of consequence.

The people of God identified with him in many ways, but they no longer lived as his people should. God says, "I won't hold anyone guiltless who empties my name of its meaning, who calls on my name but shows deep in his heart he could care less about me." Acting as if you cared about his oversight when you really don't insults God. When you do that, you say in your heart, "Phooey to you, God," and God takes that very seriously.

# Making a Name for Ourselves

One of the ways we can take the Lord's name in vain is in trying to make a name for ourselves. We may engage in activities "in the name of the Lord" with a mixed-up motivation. Instead of honestly doing it for him, we do it for ourselves. Though we talk about his name, we do it for ours.

Some people proclaim that they're doing this or that in the name of the Lord but get all bent out of shape when they don't get the glory. If they don't get a pat on the back, their noses get out of joint. If they don't get honored, they get upset because they don't really care for the name of the Lord—they care for themselves.

# Praying for Our Benefit

Though we may not have cursed since we were children and our mothers cleaned our mouths out with soap, lots of us have still taken the Lord's name in vain by praying in his name for our exclusive benefit. Someone has said that one reason we don't seem to have prayers that work is that we put all our begs in one ask-it. When we get together in our churches and tag the end of our prayers with "in the name of Jesus" or "for Jesus' sake, amen," if the prayers are all our ask-its, what have we really said? We've told God, "Hey, I want this, and I want it for me," then at the end we try to turn it around and say, "but it's really for you, Jesus." God sees through that charade.

God won't ignore it. By calling God's what isn't his at all and ignoring what *is* his, we've emptied his name of significance. Instead of putting our times and circumstances in his hands, we've tried to manipulate God to do everything our way. We've taken his name in vain while pretending to take part in one of the most powerful resources he's given us: prayer.

# Not Committing Ourselves to God's Control

When we call on God without committing ourselves to his control, we misuse his name. Members of Congress are allowed the privilege of sending their official mail free, so long as the envelope clearly states that it contains material related to congressional affairs. Some unscrupulous people have seen a way to save some bucks by printing similar envelopes for their own use. They have committed a crime in doing this, because of the abuse of the name.

It is a sobering thought that even God's servants can make false claims to be operating in his name when in actuality they are repudiating his control. Clearly there is much more involved in "taking the name of the Lord in vain" than cursing and swearing!

1.  What's in a name? What do reputation, character, personality, and authority have to do with names?

2.  What is the significance of a God who reveals his name to people, as opposed to gods that are named by people?

3.  How does the fact that you, as a Christian, bear God's name influence your behavior from day to day?

4.  Identify two subtle ways Christians use God's name in vain.

# FOUR

Remember the Sabbath day
by keeping it holy. Six days
you shall labor and do all
your work, but the seventh day
is a Sabbath to the LORD your God.
On it you shall not do any work,
neither you, nor your son or
daughter, nor your manservant
or maidservant, nor your animals,
nor the alien within your gates.
For in six days the LORD made
the heavens and the earth,
the sea, and all that is in them,
but he rested on the seventh day.
Therefore the LORD blessed
the Sabbath day and
made it holy.

Exodus 20:8-11

# 4
# This Is the Day

On Mount Sinai, the Lord God spoke these words of the fourth commandment to Moses, who passed them on to God's covenant people, the people of Israel. As a sign of their love for him, the Israelites were commanded to follow God's laws about work and leisure time. "Six days," he told them, "you shall work, and the seventh day—the leisure time—you shall keep holy."

Now we all recognize work and leisure time as integral parts of our lives, and it's encouraging to notice God has some specific words for us on this subject. We can demonstrate our relationship to the Lord by the way we work and the way we use our leisure time. These choices reflect our feelings about him.

Some folks regard work as drudgery. Every morning they drag themselves out of bed and go to work, hating every minute of it, so disgruntled they just can't wait to get to Friday and enjoy the weekend.

God's perspective on work is completely different. Work became drudgery for humankind, a necessary evil, as a result of the Fall. If you base your theology on creation, you have no case for the drudgery attitude at all. In creation God labored; therefore labor is good and right and proper. After

Adam and Eve were created, God also gave them work on the face of the earth.

The way we work will show our attitude toward God. We do better to avoid clockwatching, grumbling attitudes and to follow Paul's command, "Whatever you do, do it heartily as unto the Lord" (see Col. 3:23).

However, the fourth commandment primarily concerns leisure, not work. How are we to regard the Sabbath and keep it holy?

## Remember the Sabbath

First God says, "Remember the Sabbath day." What does that mean for us today? Obviously, we do not operate in the same circumstances as the Israelites to whom God first gave this Word. They were slaves on the run, a nomadic people newly escaped from Egypt. For them a successful day meant one in which they survived in the wilderness. They didn't even know if they would ever make it into the Promised Land.

In the twentieth century, few of us think purely in terms of survival. So how does the fourth commandment apply to today's work and leisure?

## The Inauguration of the Sabbath

God did not introduce the idea of Sabbath at Mount Sinai. Remember, he gave the Ten Commandment principles to the children of Israel before that. The miraculous provision of manna for the people as they traveled through the wilderness connected with the subject of Sabbath.

*Manna* literally means "What is it?" It simply arrived every morning, and people looked out of their tents and said, "What is it?" *Manna*. The name stuck. When mother prepared it and put it on the table, the kids did what kids always do. They turned up their noses and said, "What is it?" Mom said, "Just eat your 'What is it?' and enjoy it."

Now manna came every morning, but as soon as the sun came up, it melted away. Moses told the people to gather only enough for one day. If they took too much, it spoiled, and everybody knew they'd been greedy. But on the sixth day, they gathered twice what they needed for the day, because the Lord instructed them to do no work on the seventh day. It was to be a Sabbath unto the Lord.

In giving the fourth commandment, God confirmed the Sabbath. It's interesting to take a look at how, through the history of Israel, he amplified this idea. In Exodus 16 the Israelites are instructed not to go outside to collect manna on the seventh day. Later, when the people had become farmers and had settled down, they were told not to sow their seed or harvest a crop on the Sabbath (Exod. 34).

I grew up among many farmer friends. They went to little Methodist chapels, where I used to go preach. They would always attend, even on Sundays in harvest time. In England, harvest time is especially critical, because the country gets very little of the hot, dry weather most suitable for harvesting. So when farmers got a hot, dry day, they would drop everything, rush into the fields, and grab what harvest they could. But the old Methodist farmers refused point-blank to gather their harvest on a Sunday.

Many times I've seen it rain every day of the week and clear up on Sunday. All the unbelievers would go out and harvest their crops, laughing at the believers who left their crops standing. Those Christians operated on the basis of faith. And that's what the Lord called the children of Israel to do.

Now the Sabbath idea seemed great for the Israelite men, because they got one day in seven off, but at first they told their wives to get on with work as usual. The Lord said, "Uh-uh. No domestic activity, either." They were restricted from building fires on the Sabbath day (Exod. 35). If you go to orthodox Jewish homes today, they will not light a fire on the Sabbath. Many of them get around this rule by bringing in a Gentile to do the job, but they still adhere to that rule. What was God's point? By prohibiting fires, God illustrated the concept that the women should have the day off, too.

By the time of Jeremiah 17, the people had developed an economy; they were no longer all farming. In order to give rest to those who engaged in business, who did warehousing and trading, there are further instructions about not carrying burdens on the Sabbath day.

God simply applied the same rule to their differing situations. He says, "Six days you do your work; on the seventh day—under no exceptions—you don't work." God even commanded that Gentile strangers who lived among his people should not work either, nor shall the animals.

"Every seventh year the land shall be given a total rest as well," God says, too. "It shall lie fallow. And on the seventh of the seven-year cycle, the forty-ninth year, you will introduce the Year of Jubilee, when everything will be specially laid fallow" (see Lev. 25).

A lot of study has gone into trying to find out how we arrived at a seven-day week, and many people have come up with various ideas from different cultures. No matter what we feel about how we got a seven-day week, no other people group or culture suggested that one day in seven should remain totally free from activity. We can attribute that only to the Jewish people, and they attribute it to God and his concern for mankind.

# Why the Sabbath?

According to the fourth commandment, the Sabbath is based on creation: God created everything in six days, and on the seventh he rested. He was refreshed and reflected on all he had done. He rejoiced in all he had achieved.

But Scripture also gives three additional reasons for the Sabbath freeing people from all work activities.

## For humanitarian reasons

According to Leviticus 25, God instituted the Sabbath for humanitarian reasons. If you keep a violin strung at concert pitch all the time, it will break. People cannot keep going seven days a week. Animals cannot keep going seven days a week. Land cannot be effectively farmed year after year. If you do these things, it all falls apart. God knew this, so he ordained a day of rest.

## To show trust in God

In Deuteronomy 5, Moses reiterates the Ten Commandments as the people prepare to go into the Promised Land, exhorting the people to remember the seventh day because God brought them out of Egypt.

If these people stop working one day in seven, everybody around will say, "Are these people crazy? Are they nuts? They'll never make ends meet. They can't possibly survive." Many business people talk this way today. If you have a whole row of shops that stay open seven days a week, and one of the shop owners decides not to open, the others will say, "He's nuts. It's only a matter of time until he closes down, totally bankrupt." And that's probably what people said about the children of Israel!

God wanted his people to take off one day of the week in order to demonstrate their trust in and dependence upon the Lord. The one day in seven showed how grateful they felt toward him that on their behalf he had come through over and over again, beginning with the great blessing of their freedom from slavery under the Egyptians.

### As a sign of the covenant

Exodus 31 tells us the Sabbath is a sign of the covenant. Remember that when God made the covenant, he ordained the circumcision as its sign. This outward and visible change reflected an inward and spiritual experience. Most people know that, but do not know that the Sabbath was also a sign of the covenant.

God said, "I love you. I will be your God; demonstrate your love for me by being my people."

The people said, "How can we demonstrate our love for you?"

"By keeping my commandments."

Their obedience to this fourth commandment demonstrated their love and their position as people of the covenant.

## The Desecration of the Sabbath

As we move on through the history of Israel, we come across what Nehemiah called "the desecration of the Sabbath." The people of Israel began to abuse this one day in seven. Scripture explains this two ways.

## Lack of interest

At first, people simply used the Sabbath as a day for business as usual. In Nehemiah's time, the people of Israel had again been carried away into bondage. Subsequently some were released and found their way back into the Promised Land, Nehemiah among them. When he got back to his homeland, it became clear to this leader that the people desecrated the Sabbath day by treating it like any other day.

Their attitude demonstrated the people's utter lack of interest in worship. Although God had set aside the day, the Jews said, "We would rather do our work; we'd rather make money; we'd rather go and live our ordinary lives on this day than use it for the purpose for which God gave it to us."

Nehemiah found the people's clearly disobedient life-style appalling. Although they had an opportunity to keep this commandment, they turned a blind eye to it, demonstrating that where the rubber met the road they preferred to do their own thing rather than obey God. They demonstrated the shallowness of their covenant relationship with the Lord.

## Meticulous observance

In Christ's time we see an entirely different desecration of the Sabbath: The people became so obsessed with meticulous observation of the day that they ended up desecrating it.

How could this be? Many earnest people felt great concern about keeping the Sabbath holy. They knew they should not do work on it. They knew they could demonstrate they were not working by not carrying a burden, but they needed a definition of "work" and one of "burden."

So the rabbis got together and dealt with issues of definition on a case-by-case basis. One little old lady wanted to know if she should wear her false teeth on the Sabbath, because she thought that might constitute a burden. The rabbis duly considered it and decided those teeth were a burden, and she must not wear them on the Sabbath.

The result of all these decisions was a book called the Mishnah. People spent their lives learning these rulings and teaching them so that everyone would know what he or she could and could not do on the Sabbath. It actually came from an earnest desire to honor the Lord.

But in spelling out all the rules they got themselves in a rut. People worried about how far they could go on a Sabbath-day journey. According to the Mishnah, they couldn't go farther than a certain distance. A man might say, "But I've got to go see my mother on such-and-such a Sabbath." So before the Sabbath, he'd travel a Sabbath-day's journey, find a tree, and put food under it. He'd say, "This is my home." Then he went home. On the seventh day of the week he walked a Sabbath-day's journey to the tree, took the food, ate it, and said, "This is my home, now I can go another Sabbath-day's journey." He manipulated the law.

If he had a really long journey, he would put more food under another tree and keep working it out this way. The rules and regulations designed to help people keep the spirit of the law became an end unto themselves. Bound up by restrictions and regulations, the people lost the whole sense of loving and honoring the Lord. When Christ came, he clearly objected to all this; in effect he told them, "You are desecrating the Sabbath."

## Missing the point

In both cases, the people began missing the point God tried to make. They lost sight either by ignoring or becoming hide-bound by the rules. Now they could not play by the real ones.

Things got so bad at one point in Jewish history that on one occasion, when their enemies attacked, the people maintained, "To pick up our swords and defend ourselves would mean carrying a burden." They laid down their swords, and 1,000 of them were massacred, all because of the tight rules and regulations. God never intended this ludicrous end to his commandment.

# Clarification of the Sabbath

Jesus clarified the Sabbath by two things: his actions and his announcements.

How did he act? Scripture says in Luke 4:16 that on the Sabbath day he went into the synagogue as was his custom. In other words, Jesus worshiped regularly on the Sabbath day. He clearly and carefully adhered to this requirement.

Jesus also healed on the Sabbath. On six occasions he had monumental run-ins with the authorities over whether or not he could heal on the Sabbath. The authorities had determined that to heal was to work, and you should not work on the Sabbath, therefore healing desecrated the Sabbath. Jesus answered in this way: He said he was fulfilling the law. He was Lord of the Sabbath, and he said the Sabbath was for man, not man for the Sabbath.

What did he mean by all that? When Jesus said he had not come to set the law apart, but to fulfill it, he meant that he himself fulfilled all that the law prefigured. Because of this he was saying, "Listen, the Sabbath doesn't govern me; I govern the Sabbath."

Then Jesus said, "On that basis, remember, man was not made for the Sabbath, but the Sabbath was made for man." In other words, "In the Sabbath God graciously provides for human beings, giving man the opportunity for rest, refreshment, reflection, and the privilege of worship, obedience, and dependence. Don't get too locked in; don't swamp it with rules and regulations. Enjoy it as a precious gift from God." The Lord of the Sabbath had spoken.

# Keeping the Sabbath

How do we keep the Sabbath? Usually we simply operate on the basis of what *we* want to do, or we keep it on the basis of what tradition or upbringing insists we do. That's a far cry from thinking the rules through and coming to a conclusion before the Lord as to what we ought to do on the Sabbath day.

## From Sabbath to Sunday

A strange thing happened in Christian history. Somehow or other we got from the Sabbath to Sunday—"the venerable day of the Sun," as Constantine called it, when he legislated the first day of the week as the Lord's day.

How did we get from Sabbath to Sunday? The answer may give us a clue as to how we are to handle the Sabbath. The transitional period from the observation of the Sabbath on Saturday to the Christian celebration of Sunday has been handled differently in many ways in many parts of the world.

When Paul met with the disciples in Troas, it says they gathered together on "the first day of the week" and engaged in a worship service. When he wrote to the Corinthians, he said that when they gathered on the first day of the week, they were to bring their offerings to the Lord (1 Cor. 16). Paul makes only that one reference to the first day of the week. Scripture has relatively few of them. When we come to Revelation, John says he was in the Spirit on "the Lord's day," the only use of that term in the Scripture.

In the very early days of the Christian church the believers who were Jewish continued to worship on the Sabbath day in the synagogue. They also met on other occasions. As the Gentiles came into the church, they had no obligation to accept the Jewish Sabbath, so apparently they began to meet on other days of the week. The big question is, why the first day?

While we don't have any conclusive answers to that, we can make some inspired guesses. An obvious one is that the first day had a special quality for Christians because on that day Jesus rose from the dead. You'll also find, if you check post-Resurrection appearances, that many took place on the first day of the week. If you calculate right, you can also find that Pentecost came on the first day of the week. Among scholars, some think things began to change to the first day of the week to honor the Resurrection, post-Resurrection appearances, and Pentecost.

With so many new Gentile believers, it wasn't long before questions arose about whether Gentile believers must adhere to Jewish law. Acts 15 records that a council was called in Jerusalem. At the end, the church leaders decided the Gentiles should not follow every Jewish law, but out of respect for the Jewish people they should abstain from eating things with blood in them and adhere to one or two other minor guidelines, simply not to offend their Jewish brothers. No mention is made of observing the Sabbath day. Gentiles were not expected to follow the restrictions of the Mishnah.

By doing this, the Christian church began to move the emphasis from the seventh day of the week (the Jewish holy day) to the first day of the week. We don't know if they purposefully transferred the Jewish Sabbath to another day, with all the Sabbath entailed, or if they were saying, "We're done with the old rules, and now we enter a new era, a totally different situation."

What we believe about this question influences the way we handle the fourth commandment in our society. Today some Christians consider Sunday as the Jewish Sabbath transferred to another day, while others claim we are free from the law and in an entirely new situation.

## Sabbatarians versus Antinomians

Those who support the idea that the Jewish Sabbath has moved from the last day of the week to the first would probably agree with this statement from the Great Westminster Divines' Meeting and Assembly:

The Lord's day ought to be so remembered . . . that they [our ordinary activities] may not be impediments to the due sanctifying of the day when it comes. The whole day is to be celebrated as holy to the Lord, both in public and private as being the Christian Sabbath. To which end, it is requisite, that there be a holy cessation or resting all that day from all unnecessary labors; and an abstaining, not only from all sports and pastimes, but also from all worldly words and thoughts. . . .

What time is vacant, between or after the solemn meetings of the congregation in public, [should] be spent in reading, meditation, repetition of sermons; especially by calling their families to an account of what they have heard, catechizing of them, holy conferences, prayer for a blessing upon the public ordinances, singing of psalms, visiting the sick, relieving the poor and such like duties of piety, charity and mercy accounting the Sabbath a delight.

This document was written in England during the seventeenth century under the Puritan influence, and it described what became the traditional British Sabbath. As a result the Lord's Day Observance Society came into being, which passed considerable legislation that Britain still adheres to today. When the Puritans came over to New England, they passed similar acts that we now commonly call the "Blue Laws." This is Sabbatarianism, and it exists in several forms today.

My childhood home was Sabbatarian. We went to Sunday morning church, Sunday afternoon church, and Sunday evening church. In between those services, we played no games and could not play outside; instead we prayed or read or took part in quiet family conversations. Once my parents got a radio, they never switched it on on the Lord's day. Neither would they dream of going to a restaurant on a Sunday; that would require someone else to work.

Many earnest people are Sabbatarians. On Sunday they take no part in sports, and they believe there should be no games. They feel strongly that people should be in the place of worship, giving the day over exclusively to the service of the Lord.

The Antinomian approach contrasts entirely with the Sabbatarian one. An Antinomian simply disregards the law, and his response to it may take many forms. "We are not under law. We're under grace," such Christians might say. Really they mean, "Hey, listen. You know why those guys worshiped on Sunday instead of Saturday? They felt so relieved to get out from under the restrictive practices that were only a shadow of Christ's reality, his freedom, his love; they discovered that he would introduce them to the eternal Sabbath, and they were heading for eternal rest. When they found out about eternal rest, then they said, 'Hey, forget it. We can just be free and enjoy ourselves, relax and do whatever we wish.'" There is not much theological basis for this viewpoint, but we all know it feels good not to be required to do anything. You probably know at least a few Antinomians.

Can a solid case for either point of view be made from Scripture? Well, it depends on which Scriptures you use, which is why this remains a major controversial issue among Christians.

## Responsible Discipleship

I'd like to suggest that we neither impose rigid Sabbatarianism nor countenance irresponsible Antinomianism. Instead we should look toward developing an attitude of responsible discipleship.

What does that mean? Paul says we don't need to let anybody judge us regarding holy days or Sabbath days, that we can worship on some days as to the Lord, or we cannot worship on some days as to the Lord. Because we should honor the Lord every day, *which* day we worship together should not be a point of contention (see Rom. 14:5-6).

Now watch out! If we say, *"Every* day is special to the Lord," we may really end up living with *no* day special to the Lord. This happens when there's a job a lot of people should do. When it becomes everybody's responsibility, it ends up *nobody's* responsibility—and no one does it. It's the same with days declared holy to the Lord. Christians need to come to this point and say, "I rest in the Lord. I trust in the Lord. I obey the Lord—every single day of the week. In my secular employment, in my ordinary responsibilities, in the mundane things of life, I do them all as unto the Lord. Every day is a special one before him." Then they must live that way.

In addition, we have one very special day each week. God grants us that extra special day in order that we might use it to sharpen our focus on him and what it means to serve him, worship him, and obey him. In our society, that happens to be the first day of the week. We thank God for that day of the week and do our best not to abuse it.

When I visited Bangladesh, I discovered the Christians there worshiped on the sixth day of the week. Because Bangladesh is an Islamic state, the Muslims have decreed Friday as their Sabbath. The Christians there didn't say, "Hey, listen, we're going to work on the sixth day of the week, but we won't show up for the first day of the week." They couldn't do that. Instead they said, "Lord, it's not a matter of Sabbatarianism; it's a matter of serving you every day. If the one day happens to be the sixth or the seventh or the first or the third, it's utterly without consequence. We will take it as it comes from you and use it for your glory."

That strikes me as the right approach. We feel we should do certain things on the Lord's day. We have convictions about what we won't do on the Lord's day. That's reasonable. But do we legislate what we should and shouldn't do and legislate the actions of others? Suppose this Sunday there's a ball game. Can we go? Or if the symphony comes to town then? Should we go? How do we handle these questions?

It depends on whether you're a Sabbatarian or Antinomian, or whether you've said, "Lord, I'll tell you what I'm going to do. I'm going to take Sunday as a gift from you, and I'm going to use it responsibly. At the end of the day I'll feel very happy presenting it to you and saying, 'Lord, this was your day, and this is what I did with it.'"

If you can do that on Sunday, as you do it every other day of the week, I submit that you'll be honoring the Lord. As you honor him in this way, you'll demonstrate that you're a member of his covenant through your loving obedience to him.

1. Why is work positive and important, and not just a necessary evil?

2. Identify several examples of God's commands to the Israelites regarding the Sabbath.

3. For what three good reasons did God command his people to keep the Sabbath day holy?

4. What are three ways people desecrate the Sabbath?

5. How did Jesus shed new light on what the Sabbath was about?

6. How do you keep the Sabbath?

# FIVE

Honor your father
and your mother, so that
you may live long in the land
the LORD your God
is giving you.

**Exodus 20:12**

# 5
# Life in the Family

"Honor your father and your mother." Those well-known words seem to take a lot for granted, don't they? First they presuppose that you know who your parents are. Second, they assume you know them well enough to appreciate their significance. Finally, they imply that you have opportunity to honor them, pay them respect, and let them know how you feel about them.

But there are those who may not know their fathers and mothers. And there are those who have become so embittered against their parents, who blame them for everything that's gone wrong in their lives, that they frankly don't appreciate them. Maybe they must honestly say, "I am so out of touch with my parents that there's no way I can realistically express my appreciation to them and tell them they mean much to me."

What does it take to know our parents, honor them, and express appreciation for them? It requires an environment that fosters an ongoing, deep-rooted, interwoven relationship.

That's a family, of course. The fifth commandment talks to us about what God expects in our family living.

71

# Why Should I?

Some have responded to this commandment by saying, "Why should I honor my father and mother?" Scripture gives us at least four reasons.

In Exodus 20, God says to honor your parents "so that you may live long in the land the Lord your God is giving you" (verse 12). In Deuteronomy 5, in the parallel passage where Moses repeats the Commandments before the people enter the Promised Land, God gives the reason "that it may go well with you" (verse 16). In the New Testament Paul elaborates on these ideas. In Ephesians 6:1, he simply says you should honor them because "this is right." Finally, in Colossians 3:20 he says children should obey their parents, "for this pleases the Lord."

Why honor your parents?

It enables you to live long in the land.
It will be well with you.
It pleases the Lord.
It is the right thing to do.

There's another reason that's not in the Bible. In her book on the Ten Commandments, *Smoke on the Mountain*, Joy Davidman retells one of Grimm's fairy tales. The story tells about some parents who had both children and one grandfather living with them. Grandfather was getting a little old and sloppy. At mealtimes he tended to get his soup and porridge in places they shouldn't have gone. The parents felt concerned about this and remonstrated with granddad, but he really couldn't do anything about it.

In the end the couple didn't allow the old boy to sit at the table with the family anymore; he had to sit in the corner of the room. Joy Davidman paints a very sad picture of this old man stuck in the corner of the room in disgrace because he couldn't handle his food well. Being isolated didn't help—in fact it just allowed the situation to deteriorate until the old man couldn't eat at all. So they put his food in a trough and took away his knife, fork, and spoon; so he was made to pick up the food with his fingers and stuff it in his mouth.

The situation went from bad to worse, until one day the parents noticed the children playing in the shed. The youngsters had a saw and some wood and hammer and nails, and they seems to be building something. The parents asked, "What are you building?" The children responded, "A trough for you when you get old."

The moral of the story is, "Honor your father and mother, because one day you'll want your children to do the same to you." Your children will learn how to honor you from observing how you honored your parents.

These are good reasons for honoring our parents, but in today's society, it has become increasingly hard to live in the kind of environment that supports these rules.

## The Extended Family

Families in the Old Testament and New Testament were very different from the family we speak of today. If you look at our single-family dwelling, you immediately see what the twentieth-century person means by a family. Over the past century our single-family dwellings have gotten smaller and smaller. Why? Because the average family now has 2.4 children, a dog, and a television. That's more or less our definition of a family—we call that the "nuclear family."

The Hebrew and Greek languages don't have a word for our nuclear family; the idea is foreign to them. Each language has two words to describe family. In Hebrew one means "a wide-ranging network of blood relationships"; our word *clan* might best describe it. The second word in Hebrew means "a household of people." Joshua 7 best illustrates this for us. One of the people of Israel has done something really bad, and they have to find out who did it. So they are told to come out in their twelve tribes. Then each of the tribes divides into clans. Then each clan divides into families, and each household is questioned individually. The word for "household" is the second Hebrew word.

The Greek language conveys similar ideas. In Luke 2 it says Jesus's parents went down to Bethlehem for the census because Joseph was of the house and lineage of David. It describes the same ideas: the clan (or lineage), and the house (or household). The biblical family not only included the mother, father, and more than 2.4 children, but also unmarried aunts, widowed uncles, grandfather, and grandmother—what we commonly call the "extended family."

The biblical writers have this concept of family in their minds when they tell us to honor our fathers and mothers, because parents clearly had far-reaching responsibilities for a wide variety of relationships. Through the parents the family provided essential services.

## Economic survival

The family provided economic survival. That is how I understand the expression "Honor your father and your mother, so that you may live long in the land." The Israelites were headed for inhospitable territory, where they faced very precarious economic situations. They could only hold out by sticking together and working together for their own support.

In primitive societies today, you find the same structure of family economy. Recently I saw a film on the Gabbra tribe of Northern Kenya. Living in the inhospitable deserts of that country, their economy requires at least four people, working nine hours a day, seven days a week, just to handle the flocks. That time doesn't allow for other jobs, either. Without these four herdsmen, the tribe could not survive.

Because of this economy, the men of the Gabbra tribe cannot marry until after their mothers have reached the end of their childbearing years. When a man does marry, he cannot personally own any property whatsoever because he has to work for the family's survival.

## Emotional stability

The family also provided emotional stability. Deuteronomy 5:16 further expands this commandment to say, "Honor your father and your mother, as the LORD your God has commanded you, so that you may live long and that it may go well with you." In other words, honor *them* so that *you* may have emotional stability. The Israelites' emotional strength came from a household that held many opportunities for ongoing interaction and for a network of relationships. As part of a clan, each person gained innumerable chances to relate to others of varying backgrounds and insights.

Think of it this way. In a family of two parents and four children, there is a possibility for many relationships: husband-wife, father-son, father-daughter, mother-son, mother-daughter, brother-brother, sister-sister, brother-sister. Think of the opportunities for learning how old and young folks operate, how boys get along with boys, how girls get along with girls, and how girls get along with boys—just imagine all the combinations! It breeds emotional stability.

Add uncles, aunts, and grandparents, and throw in a few servants and some guests all living in the same household. All those extended relationships offer the possibility of increased emotional strength.

I have a theory that many people need counseling today because they have gotten away from their extended families. It used to be that the "young-timers" could get an awful lot of common-sense teaching from the old-timers. Without those extended families, today's young people have lost that depth of experience.

Families also offer a sense of belonging, a sense of identity.

## Educational structure

The family also performed a role as an educational structure. The Old Testament provided room for parent-child dialogue. It made the most of the child's delightful habit of asking questions. The child had a question, and a parent happened to be around.

Can you see the three-pronged structure that made so much sense in the Old Testament? Something had to hold everything together socially. Something had to provide economic survival, emotional stability, and educational structure. *Family* was the structure. Mothers and fathers were honorable. A person couldn't make it without them. It was as simple and basic as that.

# Today's Family

Today's family structure has shifted from the extended family to the nuclear family. The old family homes of the last century got broken up into three or four apartments, because of smaller nuclear families. And, even as houses split, we lost that broad basis of support.

The family has also moved from an emphasis on hierarchy to individuality. Instead of looking out for the good of the family, we tend to look out for the good of the individual. For instance, we send our kids out to get jobs because we say, "Work is good for you." Almost as soon as they start to work, they get their paycheck and say, "That's *my* money." They open their own bank accounts, buy their own cars. Parents don't exercise any control over the children at all.

Families today have also traded a sense of stability for modern mobility. Advanced transportation allows us to get around quickly and go far. We love to be on the move, and the idea of staying in a certain area and putting down roots actually becomes foreign. We *like* the idea of moving all the time. Families now stay in one area for an average of only three to four years.

Finally, families have also gone from an emphasis on the traditional to one on the novel. We tend to look down on "old-fashioned" things and seek "alternative life-styles." We want things to be continually fresh, new, and exciting. Over and over you hear, "That's boring," and boring means "unacceptable." We looked for something different and turned away from tradition.

## What Changed the Family?

Where do these changes come from? One cause is urbanization. In the old days people lived on the family farm or out in the deserts, or they were pioneers. In order to survive they had to hang together, because alone they could not survive. With the Industrial Revolution, people moved from the country to great urban centers, where they discovered a chance to spread their wings, do their own thing, and get away from oversight and correction. To a large extent, urbanization and industrialization destroyed the extended family.

Communication changed at the same time. In the extended family, communication and information were filtered down through the hierarchy of the family, but now anyone can listen to television or the radio or put on earphones and isolate himself from the rest of the world. What a person gets from such communications may not be in line with what his parents and his family stands for.

Today's families reap the benefits of better housing, better health, better education, better vacations, and other improvements. But those are not the only consequences of change. The family has also suffered a marked deterioration in relationships. We no longer honor parents. Instead many people lie on a counselor's couch and *blame* our parents. We don't concentrate on what they did right, but on what they did wrong.

Broken relationships become the order of the day. To a large extent, the increase in emotional disorders and the number of people experiencing emotional conflict directly result from the breakdown of our built-in societal systems.

The family currently faces all kinds of confusion concerning values. What is right? What is wrong? A young person often has a different set of beliefs from his parents'—he does things differently. As a consequence he listens to other outside voices and is influenced by them. His mother and father look at his unfamiliar behaviors and ask, "What on earth is happening?"

# Where Is the Family Going?

As we look toward the future of the family, what do we see?

People have made predictions. The pessimistic view, voiced by a world-renowned sociologist and psychologist, says the family faces extinction. The optimistic view takes the opposite side, saying, "The turbulence of tomorrow will drive people into deeper relationships." Only time will tell which will happen.

Alvin Toffler, in his book *Future Shock*, takes what I call a mediating view, combining both outlooks. He tells us, "The family will break up and shatter and it will then come together again in weird and novel ways."

Toffler may be on to something here. What does he mean by the family coming together "in weird and novel ways"? He talks about the results of new technology and what that could offer us. Before long, we could have "embryo emporiums," he says. Parents could simply go out and buy a baby. Someone else will go through the whole messy business of having the infant for them.

Sound farfetched? Maybe not. Not long ago on television I saw a program about some cattle dealers who flew to Hawaii on a chartered plane. On the way there they had a cattle auction, 37,000 feet above sea level, the highest and biggest cattle auction in the world. "How did they get all those cattle on the plane?" you might ask. They didn't, because the auction simply sold off embryos and semen. Afterwards when the interviewer asked, "What did you buy?" one man said, "Twenty semen." Another told the reporter, "Six embryos." If we have technology to do that with animals, it's only a matter of time until we have the technology to do it with humans. Once we have the technology, it won't be long before people feel we have the right to go ahead with it.

Toffler talks about the possibility of professional parents. Many couples who have two careers do not particularly want to bother with kids. We've seen this more and more. Still, they'd like to have the advantages of having children, so they'd go to a baby emporium, pay someone to have the child for them, and then send the child to professional parents, who would specialize in bringing up children. The couple would reserve visitation rights through contract.

Toffler's futuristic scenario seems unreal. But when we compare today's family to the biblical norm for a family and realize the changes that have already occurred, that future possibility doesn't seem quite so farfetched. We're considerably closer to that than we are to the biblical norm.

Toffler also mentions serial marriages. When he wrote this fourteen years ago, second and third marriages didn't happen too often. Now serial marriages are almost the norm. Toffler pointed out the difference between old-style polygamy and today's marriage style: "We have polygamy today, serially and sequentially, not contemporaneously." Instead of having a lot of spouses at once, now people just have them one after the other.

Toffler predicted that serial marriages would produce aggregate families—families of "Those are yours, and those are mine, and these are ours together," families of "semi-siblings." Contemporary sociologists and psychologists currently predict that the family is in all probability doomed.

As our culture moves farther from the old biblical norms, how can we work within the biblical principles for family? Especially if we don't even know our parents, don't know them deeply, or aren't close enough to them to express appreciation.

Any talk of honoring our parents becomes empty platitudes unless we take the changes in our society concerning marriage and the family seriously.

# Unchanging Factors in Applying the Commandment

Despite all the confusion regarding the family, some unchanging factors remain.

## *A divine origin*

The family has a divine origin. We can tinker around with "alternate lifestyles" as much as we want, but we must realize that as we move away from structural norms for society, we increase the probability of introducing uncontrollable factors. The Creator of the universe built in certain principles for the operation of families. For example, God included some ecological rules in its function. Today we readily recognize man as the biggest enemy of ecological balance, and as we become increasingly aware of this we endeavor to rectify the situation, to play by the ecological rules.

What about the damage we have done to ourselves? If we have tinkered with ecological norms and produced chaos, what have we done to our society? God ordained sociological principles, too, and we move away from them at our peril.

The beginning of Genesis records the early history of the human race. It's easy to seek that God was thinking family. Adam, Noah, Abraham, Israel—all the time God was working with the growing, extending family. It was clearly the structure of a divine ordinance. In the New Testament, Paul says he's praying to God the Father, the Father from whom every family in heaven and earth is named (Eph. 3:14-15). The Greek words for *father* and for *family* are almost identical. Paul shows the inextricable link between the Father and the family, the Father in heaven and the family here on earth. This reinforces the idea of God's ordaining the family structure.

## A divine order

Second, the family has a divine order. God clearly ordained two things: The order of the family requires that a father and mother must be honored; and the father and the mother must be honorable.

To honor father and mother means literally "to state one is deserving of respect, attention, and obedience." Isaiah told the people of Israel that God was disgusted that they "honored him with their lips but not with their hearts" (Isa. 29:13). We also face the danger of honoring our parents with our lips and not our hearts.

I must honor my parents because God ordained that my father should have a part in my protection, direction, and provision for my need. To a greater or lesser part, my father did. He may have made mistakes, but what did he do right? I honor him by acknowledging those things. My mother brought me to birth and gave me that initial care. From her I began to learn about life. If temperament is determined by the time a child reaches age six, my mother played a large role in making me the person I am. I honor her by giving her credit for the good she achieved.

You may honor your parents in many ways. When my mother was dying of cancer in England, I felt very frustrated that I could not get back to see her. We weren't sure how much longer she had. Among other things, I was finishing the manuscript for my book *What Works When Life Doesn't?* So I chose to dedicate the book to my mother. I mailed the dedication to her, and she got it the day before she died. The last thing she read from me said:

> To Mary, my mother, who brought me to life, who taught me to work, who inspired me to preach, and who, during the preparation of this manuscript, has battled cancer with quiet courage and unshaken faith, proving once again that she knows what works when life doesn't.

Take advantage of every opportunity you have for expressing the honor you feel for your parents.

In order to receive honor, parents also need to be honorable. In the New Testament Paul says, "Obey your parents," to the children. Then he says, "Parents, don't drive your children nuts." (That's my free translation of Ephesians 6:1-4.) He means that parents have a sense of divine accountability and divine responsibility. They must take their parenting so seriously before God that their children will know their parents are determined to be the parents God ordained them to be. Of course, when the parents behave honorably, children find it easy to honor them.

## A divine opportunity

The third unchanging factor is the family's divine opportunity. The family has an opportunity from God to assist those beginning to consider establishing a family. We need to help young people do it God's way. Today we get so much conflicting information about family life from the media that if we aren't confused, we aren't listening. The answer to that confusion comes from God himself.

First, though, I need to offer a word of warning. In the church some people have become so concerned about family breakdown that they focus on that to the exclusion of everything else. Others who have noticed this tendency now talk about "deification of the family" within the church.

We do need some balance. Jesus said, "Don't think I came to bring peace. I didn't. I came to bring a sword" (see Matt. 10:34). Again he told us, "The sword that I will bring will set a mother against her daughter, a father against his son, and—believe it or not—a daughter-in-law against her mother-in-law" (see Matt. 10:35-36).

What did Jesus mean? He goes on to explain, "Anyone who loves his father or mother more than me, anyone who loves his son or daughter more than me is not worthy of me" (see Matt. 10:37). In other words, Jesus said, "Don't deify the family. Don't make the family the number-one consideration. I am the number-one consideration; I am the Lord, not your kids. I am the Lord, not your family. I am the Lord, not your marriage. I will be the Lord of your children, your household, your marriage. But I will never surrender my Lordship to any or all of these things."

So if you plan to have a family, make sure you start off right. But what about families who have already started and made grave errors and for parents and children who know there are rifts in their relationships?

We should take every opportunity to give these people a new start. Some children feel deeply hurt about their parents; they may tell us about incest or physical abuse or alcoholism. They need compassionate help with their hurts and pains.

One woman called me to tell me her story. She had experienced an affair, a divorce, and remarriage to a divorced man. She and her current spouse each had children by their first marriages. Recently they had come to know the Lord. "What should we do?" she wanted to know. "Should we divorce and go back to our original partners, who also are believers and have refused to remarry?"

Although we can't always give them a fresh start, we can help these people deal with the hurts and pains of wrongdoing. We need to commit ourselves to them.

There are some things that cannot be put right. For example, there are people whose parents are gone, yet they still suffer from unresolved emotional scars, resentment, and bitterness. We must remind them that they have been forgiven if they have accepted Jesus as their Savior. Because of the forgiveness they've experienced in him, they can begin to learn what it means to forgive in his name.

Fulfilling that divine opportunity requires the power of the Spirit, the name of Christ, and the support of the body of Christ. It requires all the resources made available to us by a gracious God to become realistically involved in being a godly mother or father, grandma or grandpa, or child or grandchild in today's society. Things have changed drastically; we've gotten miles away from the biblical norm, and at our present rate of nonprogress, we'll end up thousands of miles away from it in the near future.

The Christian family becomes an example to society outside the church. The caring relationship of family could reach those who never come to church, who don't know what the Word of God says and could care less about Jesus, his cross, and forgiveness. God's plan for families could mean everything to the young couple on our street who are contemplating marriage—or who are not even bothering with marriage.

We must catch hold of the old-time principles of family and show others how those unchanging rules can work, even in a changing family scene. As we do this under God we can become an untold blessing to people who need us desperately.

1.  What are four reasons from Scripture for honoring your parents? Name one more.

2.  Describe the "family" as it was in biblical times. How have societal definitions for family shifted?

3.  What aspects of family and of God's intentions for the family have not changed?

4.  How can the Christian family become an agent of ministry to the surrounding society?

# SIX

**You shall not
murder.**

**Exodus 20:13**

# 6
# The Sanctity of Human Life

In four simple, straightforward words, God confronts us with complex ideas that require our best thinking and deepest spiritual concern.

## What Does It Mean to Kill?

In order to understand what this commandment implies, we need to comprehend the meaning of the word translated "kill" by the scholars of King James's era and "murder" by modern scholars. Hebrew has other words that could more accurately be translated "kill." This commandment does not aim at prohibiting *all* killing as much as it prohibits murder, taking life with forethought.

To clarify the issue, it helps to look at other verses that deal with similar subjects. Deuteronomy 20 gives the Bible's rules for war—and there were certainly quite a few wars in the Old Testament. How can we say the Bible says, "Thou shalt not kill," while it gives rules for war? We should understand that this chapter of Scripture places severe limits on warfare. God's people could go to war, but they could not kill women and children. There were limits on destroying life.

Exodus 21:12-13 provides minute descriptions concerning murderers and how they should be handled. Scripture clearly distinguishes between those who kill accidentally and those who kill on the basis of premeditation: Anyone who killed on purpose received capital punishment, while those who took another's life unintentionally received a different treatment. The distinction related to motive.

To care for those who killed without forethought, Numbers 35 institutes the cities of refuge. In those days if somebody had killed someone else, the police didn't come to his door because they didn't have police. And they didn't take each other to court and hire lawyers. If one person intentionally killed another, the relatives of the victim killed the guilty party. That was it. But sometimes, without vengeance or hatred, one man would slay another accidentally. In such a case the killer would go to a city of refuge before any avenger could catch him.

The city of refuge gave the killer a place to stay while others carefully looked into the facts, checked his motivations, and began the proper judicial procedures. Such cities were provided to show that the people of God differentiated between vengeful, malicious killing and accidental manslaughter. They also showed that while it was legitimate for the families of those who were murdered to kill the killer, there was no place for vigilante-style mayhem.

## In the Image of God

What rationale lies behind the command "You shall not murder"? Genesis 9:6 describes the prohibition against malicious, premeditated slaying when it says, "Whoever sheds the blood of man, by man shall his blood be shed." We call this Old Testament system *lex talionis*, "the law of retaliation." It didn't mean "an eye for an eye, and a tooth for a tooth," as some have misinterpreted. The system meant that if you take somebody else's eye, the punishment meted out to you cannot exceed the taking of your eye. The law limited the retaliation.

In the same way Genesis 9:6 provides limitation. If somebody sheds another person's blood, that first person's blood must also be shed. And the verse gives the reason: "for in the image of God has God made man."

We mustn't talk lightly about the sanctity of human life because Scripture has told us what makes human life sacred. Human life is sacred because people are made in the image and in the likeness of God.

Some people would try to tell us that a human being is a highly developed animal. Well, we would have to agree with that. When we look around at other animals, it becomes obvious that people are the most highly developed.

We all know doctors carry out experiments for medication and surgery on animals before they try them on humans. They do this because a similarity exists between us. Before men went into space, scientists sent up animals to check their reactions, which would simulate ours in many ways. We don't need to argue that man is a highly developed member of the animal kingdom. We know that.

But if someone says, "Man is only an animal," we need to argue. That statement makes it hard to support the sanctity of human life. We would reply, "Man is a highly developed animal, but God has also made man in his image."

People have differing opinions on what this means. Some say humans alone, of all the animal kingdom, are capable of conceptual thought: they can come up with ideas; they can take data and compare it with other data; they have imagination, can be creative and artistic; they can produce all kinds of things. These abilities put people in a different league from the other animals.

In addition, humankind can cooperate with the divine creative purpose. From God we have received both the mandate for the responsibility for the care and well-being of creation and moral sensitivity. About morality Mark Twain quipped: "Man is the only animal that blushes and has reason to." Truly we have a sense of what's right and wrong, what's fair and unfair, what's just and unjust. Does any other part of the animal kingdom have such sensitivity?

Finally, humankind has the ability to communicate with God and to be communicated to by him. This is a major distinctive and characteristic of our uniqueness. This communication potential will find its fulfillment in eternity, when the redeemed will share God's glory and worship him forever. Humankind has an eternal dimension.

## Challenging Divine Intention

Accordingly, when we discuss the destruction—out of vengeance or malice, on a premeditated basis—of that which God has made in his image, we're dealing with a subject of tremendous importance and concern. Destruction of what God made in his image challenges the divine intention. If God makes man for eternity and gives him the ability to function in relationship to him, anyone who kills that man destroys what God had in mind. The destroyer shakes his fist in the face of God.

Murder abrogates divine authority. If divine authority holds us in this world for a time, then takes us into eternity, the person stepping in and terminating that existence on earth tries to take the place of God. Ending human life means despising the divine evaluation. God says he has made us in his image, therefore we have profound significance. Taking life says, "I disagree, God. This person's life does not have enough significance to deserve maintaining it."

Someone has put it this way: "Man is God in effigy." We all know the anger we feel when someone gets some straw, stuffs it in an old suit, ties up the legs and arms, puts a placard on it saying, "This is the pope," hangs it on a pole, and burns it. Why do we feel upset? It's only straw, an old suit, and a pole. We get upset because that effigy speaks of the person it stands for. The actions insult the man behind the effigy.

If man is God in effigy, when we destroy man, we insult God. For that reason God prohibits the premeditated, vengeful killing of that made in his image.

# What's the Practical Relevance?

What practical relevance does the sixth commandment have for us today? I want to identify four areas in which that particular law has deep influence on us at this time in human history.

## Abortion

What does "You shall not murder" have to say to abortion?

In 1973, following the lead of the USSR and the United Kingdom, the United States passed legislation that gave a woman the right to an abortion. The lawmakers did not base that decision on the consideration of the rights of the unborn, but on the rights of the individual. Basically, they thought, a woman is an individual. She has her rights, including the right to privacy. What is more private than her body? Therefore, nobody has a right to interfere with what a woman does with her body. It sounds logical, even very reasonable. The Supreme Court agreed to that statement and enacted the law.

As a result, in the United States of America today, we have three abortions every minute, which adds up to 4,000 abortions every day. We can estimate that since 1973 fifteen million abortions have been performed in our country alone. Since the Bible states that human life is sacred, and we live in a society that quite calmly destroys fifteen million unborn children, we need to be addressing the abortion question immediately and with grave concern.

Abortion becomes a highly emotional issue. People bomb the clinics where abortions take place; they picket places where people receive abortion counseling. Some write letters to those whose children have had abortions, and all kinds of pressures are being brought to bear upon doctors who perform abortions. Meanwhile, on the other side, people level charges about right to privacy. The abortion issue is a highly publicized, highly personal, and social question. We can easily get caught up in it, and a Christian must consider how the sixth commandment applies to this issue.

The Supreme Court declared that a woman has a right to an abortion because of the privacy of her own body, but it is not an absolute right. In her first trimester, she has a right to abortion on demand, period. In the second trimester, that right remains, but the state can make regulations concerning the procedures. In the third trimester the state can, if it wishes, prohibit abortions, except when the mother's life is in some way jeopardized. So abortion is a right, but not one so broad you could drive a tank through it.

The sixth commandment categorically forbids us to destroy that which is made in the image of God. If we decide that the child in the womb is made in his image, then abortion is horrendously wrong.

As Christians we look to the Bible to decide what status we should confer upon the fetus. Exodus 21:22 describes a situation in which two men fight and cause a woman to give birth prematurely, but she suffers no serious injury. The offender, Scripture says, must be fined whatever the husband demands and the court allows. People have interpreted this in various ways.

Some say that it means that if, through the men's struggling, she accidentally miscarries, no suggestion is made that the life of the offender should be laid down on the basis of blood for blood and life for life. Those arguing this way claim that Scripture does not consider the fetus a human being, because if it did, it would demand the life rather than the fine.

Jeremiah 1:4-5, however, describes the prophet's experience. He says: "The word of the LORD came to me, saying, 'Before I formed you in the womb I knew you, before you were born I set you apart; I appointed you as a prophet to the nations.'" God doesn't describe Jeremiah as an accident in the womb. God formed Jeremiah in the womb and knew him before his birth. Even before Jeremiah's birth, God had set him apart as a prophet.

Psalm 139:13-16 makes similar powerful statements. "For you created my inmost being; you knit me together in my mother's womb. I praise you because I am fearfully and wonderfully made; your works are wonderful. . . . My frame was not hidden from you when I was made in the secret place. When I was woven together in the depths of the earth, your eyes saw my unformed body. All the days ordained for me were written in your book before one of them came to be."

In the New Testament, we discover the lovely story of Mary, who was told she would bear the Messiah and then went to see her cousin Elizabeth, who was already pregnant. When Mary makes the announcement, the unborn John the

Baptist leaps in Elizabeth's womb; he recognizes the miracle that has taken place.

The Bible certainly says the unborn one is capable of relationships, of some sort of spiritual insight, and of receiving some sort of divine purpose. It specifically states that God forms it. Some people therefore say that what is in the womb is from the moment of conception made by God and falls under the principle of the sixth commandment. Under no circumstances at all must we harm it.

Physicians have given us a wide variety of suggestions about when the fetus becomes human. Seven of them are outlined by Oliver O'Donavan and quoted in Norman Anderson's *Issues of Life and Death*.

1. The first group says the fetus becomes fully human at the point of conception. Among those some would say "the point of conception" rather unguardedly, while others would describe it not as a moment, but a process that we cannot accurately measure. But both would agree that, whenever it takes place, the child becomes invested with the divine image.

2. Others claim that the problem with the first theory is that 50 percent of all impregnated ova disappear in the natural course of events. If that is the case, then 50 percent of unborn, unformed, unimplanted ova have the divine image and simply drift off into eternity without having existed in any sense that is meaningful to us. These people state that the person starts to be formed at implantation; before that it has no meaningful existence at all.

3. A third group says the fetus becomes human when it takes human shape. They say it will measure at least three

centimeters, which will happen between forty-five and forty-nine days after conception.

4. Still another group claims the fetus becomes human at animation. Old-time theologians used to try to figure out when the body got the soul and when the soul left. They thought of the body having a soul, as opposed to thinking that humans are body, soul, and spirit. When it came to animation, people believed—and in some circumstances still do believe—that a time exists when the fetus becomes ensouled. To give you an idea how things have changed, Aristotle said that took place twenty-five to forty days after conception for the male, but fifty to eighty days after conception for the female.

5. A fifth way of thinking says the fetus becomes human at viability—the point at which it could survive without its mother. We have a problem with this today because with our rapidly advancing technology the fetus's viability point changes all the time. Supreme Court Justice Sandra Day O'Connor said, "Fetal viability in the first trimester of pregnancy may be possible in the not too distant future." If that happens, it will make the Supreme Court's ruling palpable nonsense.

6. Another set of people would try to get the problem out of the way simply by declaring the fetus human at birth, not before. If so, how do you take into account the biblical passages we've considered?

7. Finally, some would claim that the fetus becomes fully human one year after birth. They say that at this stage the human child is comparable to all other animals at the

moment of birth, because human children are much more helpless than other animals.

All this speculation leaves us in a great, big fog—because when we look at Scripture, medical science, and our knowledge, we find it very difficult to pinpoint the moment the unborn becomes a human made in the image of God.

Because of this difficulty, people argue about whether the fetus is a person, is fully human, is subhuman, or is potentially human. Those in favor of aborting call it subhuman. They would compare it to an appendix—simply a pile of useless tissue, lacking importance. In the light of Scripture, we cannot accept this position under any circumstances.

Despite the complexity of the issue and the degree of uncertainty that surrounds it, if we allow the fetus to go full term, it *will* become a human being. Therefore under no circumstances should we feel comfortable in agreeing to any callous or careless interference with that. If I cannot categorically say *when* something is made in God's image, I'm not even going to get close to tampering with it. It would seem we need to take that minimal position at the very least.

If we are in favor of life, we must favor not only the life of the unborn, but also that of the mother. We need to express concern for the mother, her physical well-being, her emotional situation, and her spiritual state.

We need to care for the young woman whom we tell, "In having an abortion, you murdered something made in the image of God." What will that do to her emotions? How does that affect her spiritually? How can she look the world in the face again?

If we aggressively go after women who have had abortions, we may well drive them to the point of emotional breakdown or even suicide. Among those who have experienced abortions, there exists a high incidence of depression and an increasingly high level of suicide. It seems to me that if we call ourselves prolife, we must be prolife for the unborn and the born as well. We've got to be for the fetus and for the mother, which complicates the abortion issue quite dramatically.

In some cases that means we must balance out the rights of the unborn against those of the living. The Roman Catholics have arrived at a simple answer for this: They see the rights of the fetus as the primary ones. Those in the feminist tradition and with more liberal thinking call that nonsense, saying the rights of the living are far more important than the rights of the potentially living. Others who grapple with the Word of God ask, "How do we put these together?"

Can we countenance abortion on demand? Emphatically no! Can we ban abortion, period, for all circumstances and conditions? It would seem to me that by doing so we could get ourselves in situations where we cannot adequately deal with the needs for the life of the mother and the life of the unborn. Some people would probably agree that if the mother has a very major medical problem, and carrying the child threatens her life, action needs to be taken. To balance this out, let me quote a British physician: "In forty years of gynecological and obstetric practice, I can only remember a handful of occasions in which the mother's life was in danger because of the birth of the fetus." We need to bear that in mind.

I believe we must uphold the sanctity of life for both the born and the unborn. I believe we must take that position. If we wish to take a stand for the rights of the unborn, potentially made in the image of God, we must be ready at the same time to care for those who have had abortions and feel depression and overwhelming guilt and who might commit suicide. We need to cultivate compassion for both. When we persuade women not to abort the unborn, we should be prepared to help with the steps of the pregnancy that follow. But we also need to aid those who need forgiveness—we must help human lives in many dimensions, not only in the right to be born.

## Suicide

Today we have a major problem with suicide among young people. It is estimated in the United States of America that 5,000 young people kill themselves every year—a 300-percent increase since 1960.

People view suicide differently. We all know of the heroic approach of the Japanese kamikaze pilot. And we've seen the Romeo and Juliet romantic view where young lovers can't marry but can't bear to be apart, so they end it all together. Then there's the pessimistic approach that comes from the depths of depression, particularly with young people who lack an adequate support system to deal with difficult emotions.

The command, "You shall not murder" must clarify our position on suicide. Killing oneself seems to be the worst kind of murder. Do we agree with the ancient church that would refuse to give a suicide a Christian burial?

On the other hand, we can't simply shrug our shoulders and pretend that suicide doesn't matter. There is something heinously wrong about suicide because it usurps divine prerogative, destroying something of intrinsic worth. In committing suicide, a person also says to humanity, "I think you are not worth being a part of." As G. K. Chesterton said, "Suicide is the refusal to taken an interest in existence; it insults everything on earth."

Christians must take a strong stand on the suicide issue. Destroying that which is made in the divine image—particularly yourself—is fundamentally wrong. Having said that, we must caringly approach suicidal people to provide the missing support system, to become family, to find healing for depression, to help bear the burdens.

In other words, if we're for the sanctity of life, let's make sure we don't just make the negative statement, "You shall not murder," but that we also make a positive statement by reaching out to those in all kinds of troubled circumstances.

## Capital punishment

This sixth commandment affects the Christian's perspective on capital punishment as well. The Bible seems to accept it as a normative approach. Genesis 9:6 clearly states that whosoever sheds the blood of man, by man shall his blood be shed because people are made in the image of God.

Today many people appeal to the Old Testament, saying Scripture requires capital punishment. Further, they tell us, the punishment fits the crime: If somebody takes it into his hands to destroy something made in the image of God, we can only demonstrate the seriousness of the act by making him pay the supreme penalty—his life.

Moreover, claim the capital-punishment advocates, we need deterrents; if we take the life of every murderer, the rest of society will know they'd better respect life. Society needs protection from murderers, they remind us, and if we get rid of them, we're certainly protected from them.

People concerned about criminals agree a punitive aspect must exist—people need a deterrent, and society needs protection. But there's another point of view that asks, "Shouldn't steps be taken for the remedy of the criminal, for a restoration to some degree of normalcy? How can that take place if the person is destroyed through capital punishment?"

Some feel that the time between the sentence and the execution adequately allows for restoration. One person put it this way: "One good thing about capital punishment—about the death sentence—is it wonderfully focuses the attention." And it's true that there are those on death row who get their acts together before they are executed.

Though we may call for this Old Testament principle today, we must not apply it across the board. The Old Testament prescribed capital punishment not only for murderers, but also for homosexuals, and for unruly teenagers. That's how you handled your delinquency problems back then—you killed them. So if we argue for capital punishment, on what grounds do we decide where it applies and where it doesn't? Do we execute blasphemers? Do we execute homosexuals? Do we execute juvenile delinquents? Or do we execute only murderers? If we go ahead and apply capital punishment on the basis of the Old Testament Scripture, is this not an uneven application?

We can easily recognize how open capital punishment is to abuse. For instance, of all those people tried for murder, 80 percent of the blacks received convictions, compared to 60 percent of the whites. Not only do we face the possibilities of error and bias, we open ourselves to the possibility of the callousing of society when we apply the death sentence. Such punishment certainly brutalizes the people involved in the execution.

Recently I saw an example of this in the story of an elderly lady executed in North Carolina. A very dear friend of mine visited this woman—the first to be executed in many years in the United States—while she was on death row. They became firm friends. The woman on death row had become a believer and had a prisonwide ministry. Although many others made appeals on her behalf, the governor of the state did not pardon her.

As the execution date neared, the prisoner became more apprehensive. My friend asked, "Would it help you in any way if I were present at your execution?" The woman welcomed what she felt would be a tremendous help to her, knowing that my friend was there praying for her at that moment and said yes.

My friend went and witnessed the execution. Five days afterwards she called me to say, "I have gone through the most excruciating thing imaginable. I can't think straight. I can't sleep. The execution keeps replaying in my mind like a bad dream. I feel I am on the verge of coming apart. Please help me."

My friend is one of the most godly, most gifted, most capable people I know—one, in fact, who supports capital punishment. But she found it exceptionally difficult to witness an execution.

As far as I'm concerned, if I am in favor of capital punishment, presumably I'm in favor of doing it myself. If I'm not in favor of doing it myself—which I'm not—why not? Maybe I have that sense of uneasiness because I wonder if I can be so right before God that I can clearly and absolutely know all the facts and factors and feel free to take that life. I don't ever think I could arrive at that position. Could you?

## War

As we consider the command not to kill, we ultimately come to the issue of war. An activist approach says, "If the government says I've got to do it—I have to defend the shores of my homeland—then I'll do it. And I'll do it under any circumstances."

The pacifist positions vary, but many of them say, "Jesus said we should not retaliate, that those who live by the sword

103

will perish by the sword. I absolutely cannot justify it. The way to handle things is the way of the cross, and I would rather die than make someone else die."

In between lies the selectivist approach: "Under some circumstances war is justified, and when that is the case, I will feel I can participate."

Saint Augustine introduced the idea of a just war. This doctrine has been in vogue down through the years. If you were raised in the thirties in England, as I was, you knew the meaning of a just war. It meant beating Hitler and the Nazis. There was no problem with that. Everybody felt very patriotic and marched off—they couldn't wait to get into uniform and have a go at the Hun.

As time went on, though, we discovered that we had bombed Dresden, which had no military value whatsoever, and we wiped it out. Then we found out we had bombed Hamburg, obliterating thousands of civilians. We justified it as retaliation for the bombings of London and Coventry. But some of us began to ask, "Where's the justice? Isn't it getting out of hand?"

When America dropped the atom bomb on Hiroshima, we became even more concerned. In just a flash the explosion ushered more than 70,000 people into eternity. When the statistics came out, we noticed that as a result of World War II, in Europe alone, 20 million Russians lost their lives. Six million Jews were exterminated; 6.5 million Germans lost their lives; 1 million Allies died. Many of us began to ask: "What is this just war?" Can we really justify more than 30 million people in Europe alone being exterminated like that? Were there things so important that they justified the taking of lives made in the image of God?

Many people began to ask some hard questions—ones that got even harder when Vietnam came along. In that conflict 4 million Vietnamese died, and about 58,000 Americans lost their lives. We began to ask, "What is the justice? Where is the rightness in this thing?" People became much more concerned about war.

Now we've moved away from the war concept, into weapons buildup. On this earth we have the equivalent of four tons of TNT for every man, woman, and child alive. If you thought Hiroshima was bad, let me tell you about the Poseidon submarine, which has sixteen missiles on board, every one with ten warheads. At the height of the Cold War every Poseidon submarine targeted 160 Soviet cities, and each warhead had the capability of three times the power of the Hiroshima bomb. Now with the collapse of the U.S.S.R. we face the unnerving possibility that new nuclear arsenals could become available to the highest bidder. Some people are so scared they are almost nostalgic for the good old days of the Cold War!

Now we confront a situation where we have the ability to destroy the earth over which God has made us stewards. We must ask ourselves, In this situation do I have the freedom to move along with my society, or do I stand against it? Do I believe some principles that come from Scripture, which are so profound that I must wrestle with them?

Christians must engage in some really hard thinking about war, capital punishment, euthanasia, suicide, infanticide, abortion, and all the other life-and-death issues. We've got to apply the Ten Commandments to our day seriously.

People don't really want to wrestle with these issues. In my church's study center we ran a course on Christian ethics, and hardly anyone applied. It seems to me that how the sixth commandment applies to believers today should trouble our minds.

Remember, when the Lord Jesus picked up on this issue in the Sermon on the Mount, he said, "Listen, if you kill somebody, they'll hold you before the Sanhedrin for judgment. But I'll tell you something worse than that. If you hate someone in your heart, if you're malicious, if you insult people, if you wish them dead, if you want them out of the way, if you say they're worthless, if you deny that they are what God says they are, you're not in danger of the Sanhedrin; you're in danger of hell itself" (see Matt. 5).

Jesus escalated and pinpointed the problem, which lies in our hearts. Every single one of us is capable of bitterness and hatred, of selfishness. As we begin to look at our own hearts, we might become concerned about the possibilities there.

## Overcoming Evil

What rules of thumb can we apply to dealing with this life-or-death issue? Romans 12:9 tells us, "Hate what is evil." Is there anything evil in the war issue, the capital punishment issue, the abortion issue? Well, don't just sit there—hate it!

If you hate evil, seek to overcome it! Don't stand by uninvolved. But be careful, "Do not repay anyone evil for evil" (Rom. 12:17). If we handle evil with evil, we simply compound it. Romans 12:9 continues, "Cling to what is good." We need to handle evil with good. How do we handle nuclear proliferation? Not with more evil. Do we handle the abortion issue by bombing clinics? No. We need to recognize that evil has to be hated, but we must overcome it with good. And I don't believe that is naive in light of today's complex political situations.

In Romans 13 Paul simply and straightforwardly describes the government's role in this: It's there to reward those who do good and punish those who do evil. When government fails to do the task God appointed it to accomplish, when the government does evil, we must hate it. We stand against it, and we seek to overcome it with good.

What happens if evil leaders refuse to turn around and take the side of good? We cannot sit by and say, "It's my country, right or wrong." We will respond, "There's no way we're going to sit idly by and let that happen." Because we understand the sanctity of human life and know that God made us in his image, I hope we can stand up for what we believe. We can't afford to feel differently about humanity from the way God feels about it.

As we consider the meaning of the destruction of life made in God's image, as we face the issues of abortion, suicide, capital punishment, and war and seek to do something about them in our world, "You shall not murder" will require a great work of grace in our hearts. Before we may put the commandment into operation, we must turn to God for forgiveness, deep love, and the power to confront evil with good to change our world.

As God told the Israelites to live by the Commandments to show their love for him, so he tells us to do. "If you love me," he calls, "obey my commandments."

1. What makes human life sacred? What makes it different from the life of animals?

2. How does the command not to kill affect your perspective on the issue of abortion? If sanctity of life applies to both the born and the unborn, what is the Christian's responsibility to unwed mothers and those who have had an abortion?

3. How does your position on the sanctity of life push you to protect or help those who feel suicidal?

4. Are you for or against capital punishment? Should the Christian be concerned for those who are required to terminate life under capital punishment?

5. Describe your position on the Christian's involvement in war. Does "hating what is evil" sometimes require war?

6. Is it naive to believe that Christians can overcome evil with good in our society? Why or why not?

# SEVEN

You shall not
commit adultery.

Exodus 20:14

# 7
# Preserving the Sanctity of Marriage

Often people will tell you they feel turned off by the Ten Commandments. "All those 'thou shalt nots,'" they complain. "Who wants to hear it?" We all share that emotion to some degree. As soon as somebody says, "You shall not," something in our human nature cries, "Oh, yes, I shall!"

The other day I saw a sign that said *Do Not Enter.* Immediately I felt a desire to enter there. I responded to the *negative.*

Then I saw the word *Explosives,* and I realized they had a good reason for the negative command. Behind that sign lay the positive message, "We are concerned for you."

The same is true with the Ten Commandments. They seem so negative that we don't much like them. However, just as in the case of that sign, we have to realize that positive statements lie behind the negative ones.

The seventh commandment shows God's deep concern for the sanctity of marriage. God knew that nothing could destroy a marriage—that beautiful thing ordained by him—

more quickly than adultery. So God said, "Thou shalt not" with a positive intention.

Twentieth-century Christians aren't the only ones who have problems with this commandment. Scripture clearly shows that the ancient cultures had problems with sexual immorality. Among the prophets, Jeremiah struck out at adulterous relationships with attention-getting words that described his contemporaries as stallions neighing after their neighbors' wives. The apostle Paul, ministering to the Corinthian church, complained, "There's an unspeakable thing going on in Corinth—you've got sexual immorality so gross I don't even want to talk about it. Yet you folks not only condone that sin, you pride yourselves on being a great church!"

When the Lord Jesus ministered, he talked about adultery in unexpected terms. He said, "If you lust after somebody, that's like committing adultery in your heart." In addition he described the flippant approach to divorce, so common in his day, as simply legalized adultery.

The Lord Jesus, the apostles, and the prophets all decried the insidious, pervasive problem of sexual immorality. God spoke through them because he felt concern that marriage, his fundamental structure of society, was coming apart at the seams.

Some people would say that today we live in the greatest society and culture on earth. Frankly, I don't know where they're looking. Because if we look honestly at our society, comparing it to the ancient cultures that were fractured and fragmented, we see that we face the same danger. To combat that, we've got to consider what God says in his concern for preserving marriage.

# The Curse of Adultery

I call adultery a curse for six good reasons.

## Defying God

First, adultery defies God. He says, "You shall not commit adultery." Every time a person commits this sin, he or she openly goes against what God says.

Remember the story of Joseph, who was a slave down in Egypt working for a gentleman named Potiphar? Potiphar went traveling, and while he was gone he entrusted his house and business to young Joseph. Repeatedly Mrs. Potiphar tried to seduce Joseph, but the young man always resisted. One day while her husband as away, she tricked Joseph into a compromising position and suggested they engage in an adulterous act. He answered, "Your husband has committed everything into my care. He entrusted it all to me. How could I abuse that trust?" Then he went a step farther, "How can I abuse that trust and sin against God?" (see Gen. 39:8-9).

Kind David got himself in a compromising situation and responded differently. He ended up committing adultery and even murder. When Nathan the prophet confronted and challenged the king, David repented and said to God: "Against you, you only have I sinned. And you are absolutely just and right in judging me" (see Ps. 51:4).

Both David and Joseph finally understood that adultery fundamentally defies God. That in itself ought to be enough for us, but being what we are, we need to know other reasons why adultery is a curse.

## Destroying families

Second, adultery destroys families. God has a commitment to the family. When he reiterated the law in Deuteronomy 6, just before the children of Israel would leave the wilderness and enter the Promised Land, he did so in the context of the family. He said, "I have given you these laws and these commandments and these decrees for you, your children, and your children's children."

God gave the law in the context of a healthy family. From the very beginning he expressed his concern for the reproduction of human life through the family; he clearly stated that marriage and family are his way of doing things.

Adultery destroys the sacredness, uniqueness, and specialness of marriage, the basis on which families are built. Recently a woman wrote to me about the troubles adultery had brought to her family. Because she and her husband had taken a strong stance against their son's relationship with a married woman, they had lost the affection of all their children. The others had sided with him, against the parents' acceptance of God's Word about this sin.

As a result of their son's adultery, this couple experienced great anguish; they saw their family fall apart. Unless we want such situations to become even more common than they are today, we have to agree with God, because if we don't say what he does about adultery, we're dead wrong. Our society shows it.

## Defiling marriage

Third, adultery defiles marriage. From the beginning God made it clear that when a man and woman come together, he makes them one. If two people come together, joined by God, publicly making a covenant and commitment to each other, then and only then do they have the freedom under God to consummate that union. They demonstrate their oneness by becoming one flesh. In simple terms it means that when two bodies come together in sexual union, that in itself is the pinnacle of their joining together by God. To consummate a union that is no union is a lie. To consummate it before it's a union is a sham. For that reason we must insist on the wrongness of sex outside of marriage. We must stand unequivocally at this point.

Now if two people marry, and one decides to take sexual union outside that relationship, that person defiles what God has joined together. Over and over in the marriage ceremony we stress the commitment God requires: "Wilt thou have this woman [this man] to be thy wedded wife [husband], to live together according to God's ordinance in the holy state of matrimony? . . . Wilt thou love, comfort, honor and keep her [him] in sickness and in health? And forsaking all others, keep thee only unto her [him] so long as you both shall live?" The answer to each is "I will."

If either the bride or groom does not answer, we have no marriage. Any married person has to understand that he or she has made a solemn covenant in the presence of God, which has joined them together. Only then may they consummate that union by sexual activity. To do so outside the marriage bond defiles the concept of marriage itself.

## Denying love

Fourth, adultery denies love. People in our modern generation will tell us that they engage in affairs because they love each other. Now who outside the relationship can dispute that? Certainly they must share some degree of affection, unless it's a one-night stand. An ongoing relationship presumably contains some kind of love, but love comes in many shapes and forms.

New Testament Greek has three words to describe love. *Eros* means "erotic love." *Phileo* describes the love of companionship. *Agapē* indicates the love of commitment, love that says, "I'm concerned primarily with your well-being."

Now people can surely get into an adulterous relationship where they share marvelous eros. Others may get into one where the companionship is better than they get at home. But these people do not love each other as they should before God, for one simple reason. If two people love each other with agapē love, a total commitment to each other's well-being envelops and enriches them.

To put it more bluntly, suppose as a pastor I engaged in an adulterous relationship with one of the ladies of my fellowship, and people in the congregation came and said to me, "Stuart, you shouldn't do this. It is not right. We can't have it."

"But we love each other, and love is of God," I might reply. "The Commandments say that we should love one another." How could my congregation respond? Could they tell me we did not love each other? Quite possibly we could share an erotic attraction. Companionship and compatibility could exist. But we could not share agapē, because agapē is a commitment to what God says and to the well-being of that other person. If that lady had a husband, how could I consider her well-being yet fracture her marriage? What about my wife, Jill, and my children? If I am really loving, I am concerned primarily with their good, not my own.

When people in adulterous relationships say, "We love each other," they probably do at a superficial level, but they cannot say, "We love each other in the sense God has

116

ordained we should truly love." Adultery cannot show you're concerned primarily for others—it denies love as it really is.

## Deriding faithfulness

Fifth, adultery derides faithfulness. God has leaned out of heaven and agreed to be our God and invited us to become his people on the basis of covenant, the essence of which is faithfulness. God says, "I will be faithful to you; be faithful to me. Demonstrate that faithfulness by dealing faithfully with others according to my instructions."

The Old Testament writers used the same concept of covenant to hit us with great force. Proverbs 2:17 talks about the woman who seduces a man as follows: "[She] has left the partner of her youth and ignored the covenant she made before God." If I engage in adultery, faithfulness to my wife and to God has fled.

As soon as someone has been unfaithful in one area, he can become unfaithful in many areas. If we want to stand for reliability, faithfulness, and commitment, we must prove those qualities in our marriages and remain true to our vows. Our marital faithfulness will begin to spread to other areas of faithfulness.

## Degrading people

Sixth, adultery degrades people. Romans 1:24 tells us that because of the attitude of the wicked, God has just let them go all the way into all kinds of sexual immorality and impurity. As a result, they have degraded their own bodies. We're all painfully aware of this tendency today.

Adultery can cause terrible physical damage. The AIDS epidemic is terrible proof. People can no longer sit back comfortably and say, "Well, AIDS is just a homosexual disease; it couldn't happen to me." The disease is already spreading rapidly into heterosexual relationships as a result of today's rampant sexual promiscuity.

Adultery also spreads venereal disease: gonorrhea, syphilis, and chlamydia (which scientists estimate may infect up to 10 million new people this year).

Not only do adulterous relationships expose people to physical damage, they also take a heavy emotional toll. To give yourself in the fullest possible way and to discover that you've been taken for a ride causes serious emotional scarring. Discovering your spouse has betrayed you and your vows shatters your psyche.

What then of the communal impact of adultery? One eminent historian recently concluded a study of the rise and fall of civilizations. About his research he said, "After a study of eighty-eight civilizations, I have come to the conclusion that a human society is free to choose either to display great energy or to enjoy sexual freedom. The evidence is that they cannot do both for more than one generation."

In other words, tell American society it has a choice: Engage in sexual freedom, or expend energy that will produce a superlative community. We can't do both. If we continue in the way we're going, we may have to accept that our society faces the direst of dangers. Adultery degrades people—physically, emotionally, communally, culturally, and spiritually.

The apostle Paul puts it this way: "Your body is the temple of the Holy Spirit, and how can you take that and join it in unfaithfulness?" (see 1 Cor. 6:19). How can you take the unique property of God and engage in actions that are the antithesis of all he stands for?

# Causes of Adultery

In standing against adultery, I do not mean to sound insensitive—adultery does have causes that come from deep problems, of which I can outline four.

## *Uncertain standards*

Uncertain standards open the door to adultery. Whether or not we know it, we act on the basis of what we believe. Our philosophy forms the basis of our lifestyle. If we know what we believe, we will know what we should do. When we have doubts about our beliefs, we feel uncertain about how we should act.

God realizes we all need some rules to play by, and he gives them to us. In the area of sexuality, he states two divine principles quite clearly: no adultery; no fornication.

The Old Testament defined *adultery* as "sexual intercourse by a man with a married woman who is not his wife." Notice that left a lot of room for married men to engage in intercourse with unmarried women without its being called adultery. This double standard came from the way the people regarded women—as property, not persons. That's why the Tenth Commandment says, "You shall not covet your neighbor's possessions" and included a man's wife. She was considered his property.

Through the ministry of Christ and the apostles, the position of women became tremendously upgraded. As women received greater freedom and status, they demanded a change in the definition of adultery. Now we see adultery defined as "sexual immorality between two married people who are not married to each other." But don't let this give you the idea that it gave single people the freedom to have sex. They just had another word for it. In Greek, *porne*, from which we get the word *pornography*, means "fornication," and it describes illicit sexual activity between unmarried people. The Bible doesn't act squeamish about any of this. With its straightforward standards it condemns it all openly.

Alongside these standards—and in direct contrast—are our contemporary mores. Compared to the "thou shalt nots," they seem considerably more attractive, especially when the philosophies are phrased in inviting terms. Those who advocate all kinds of sexual liaisons say, "Listen, we're into honesty rather than hypocrisy. We know all these people who go to church—we know what goes on behind their pious behavior. We're not like that; we're not hypocrites. We're honest." And we might think, *Wow, hey, that's good. Based on these mores, our contemporary society won't produce hypocrites; it will produce real, honest people*. But as we begin to scratch the surface, though, we find that in these circumstances "honesty" is just another name for hypocrisy!

Someone who supports such standards may say, "I have a meaningless relationship at home, but this one is meaningful." *Meaningful* sounds fantastic but means nothing. What about the meaning of *spouse* and *child?*

He might also talk about maturity. "We're not going to have this back seat stuff; we want to behave as responsible adults. Instead, we want to be mature about this. We look the world in the face and say, 'Hypocrites, we are responsible adults.'" Yet these "mature" people destroy spouses and children wherever they go.

## Unrestrained sexuality

Unrestrained sexuality also causes people to get into adultery. Obviously, God gave us a sex drive. He wanted the world populated, and he knew how to do it in a way that would give us great pleasure. Sex drive is phenomenal. But everybody knows that any healthy male could populate a small town, given the chance, so we've got to stop him. There have to be limits placed on him.

God also invented fire, which can get out of hand. He created water, which can flood. He made all kinds of things that, unless they're guarded, may cause us trouble. The God who created our sex drive also placed the limits on it, too, but we don't want to accept them.

Where do we find the limits on sex today? The media glamorize and sensationalize it. Peer pressure tells us to go ahead.

With considerable insight C. S. Lewis said: "There are people who want to keep our sex instinct inflamed in order to make money out of it because a man with an obsession is a man who has very little sales resistance."

As we confront all manner of pressures about our sexuality, unless we have set solid standards, unrestrained sexuality will sooner or later overcome us, producing fornication or adultery.

## Unfulfilled desires

A lot of people today have unsatisfactory marriages. Not so long ago we'd say to such couples, "Tough it out!" But in the last few years attitudes have changed considerably. If a man has an unsatisfactory marriage and can't face going home to the noisy kids, a griping wife, and a house that looks like a bomb has recently dropped, he doesn't have to. Instead he can have a "meaningful relationship" during happy hour over civilized drinks with some attractive woman. He'd be crazy to go home to that disaster area when he could have one quiet, relaxing hour, he decides. He has an unsatisfactory marriage, unfulfilled desires, and unlimited opportunities. He takes those opportunities, and that's how adultery happens.

Sometimes men in middle age hit a midlife crisis and begin to feel unsure about how attractive they are, whether they still have what it takes. The temptation exists to find out by trying someone younger. And women do the same thing with younger men.

Why does adultery happen? Because people have unsatisfactory marriages and unlimited opportunities. They feel lonely, unsure, insecure, unappreciated. When they find someone who cares, appreciates them, and looks really neat, they start a "meaningful, mature relationship"—and they're on the slippery slope to disaster.

## Undisciplined lifestyles

Jesus says, "If your eye offends you, pluck it out. If your right hand offends you, cut it off. It's better to enter into life missing a limb or two than to enter hell with your body intact, isn't it?" That seems like powerful logic. It's also hyperbole.

Some of the early church fathers took those words seriously. One made himself a eunuch because he took Christ's words literally in his struggle with sexual desires. Yet what Christ actually meant was, if you're going to avoid getting into an illicit sexual relationship, discipline your life. Don't pluck your eye out; cancel your subscription to *Playboy*. Stop putting your hand in your pocket to pay for certain channels on your cable TV. Pornography is a $2 billion business in America today. Why does it rake in so much cash? Because it has so many customers—many of them sitting in your church on a Sunday morning—demonstrating an undisciplined lifestyle.

With such an uncurbed way of life, in time, unfulfilled desires and their unrestrained sexuality built on uncertain standards will lead inevitably into illicit sexual relationships—in thought if not in deed.

## So What Now?

I do not want to suggest that extenuating circumstances do not exist. They do. I understand the bad marriages, the loneliness, the insecurity, and all the other things that can drive a person toward that illicit romance. But I also realize that the lack of standards, undisciplined lifestyle, and unfulfilled desires create an explosive mix. As a pastor, I've been on hand to pick up the pieces over and over again.

Why do we fall into such situations? Sometimes it's just because we won't call sin "sin." We substitute all sorts of polite words that make our behavior seem less bad, so we can live with it, because we don't want to attack it head-on. Where have we gone wrong?

We can't stop the sexually attractive things that go on around us, the stuff that bombards our ears and minds through TV and billboards. But Martin Luther had a good word on this: "You can't stop the birds from flying over your head, but you can sure stop them from nesting in your hair." If we begin to call our lust and desire, which we've nurtured and fed, "sin," deep in our hearts we'll begin to understand the attractiveness of this sin and learn to avoid it.

## Cure for Adultery

How do we stop adultery? We have two cures: preventive medicine and remedial medicine. If you have a choice, go for the preventive kind!

## *Preventive medicine*

How do we prevent adultery? We agree with God on what he says on the subject, and we love what he says. Second, we recognize the necessity to grow in grace. Colossians 3 and Galatians 5 contrast the works of the Spirit to those of the flesh. God requires us to live in his Spirit, not on the basis of our fleshly desires. We need to agree with him about the importance of walking with him.

Once we have agreed with God and have begun to nurture our spiritual lives, we can develop healthy families based on our nurturing of our loved ones' spiritual lives. This includes a healthy sexual relationship in marriage, because you can't have a healthy marriage if the sexual relationship is not strong. So agree with God on what he says. Say, "I believe. I stand on it." Build into your life a spiritual growth in grace. Put off the old things and put on your new life in Christ. Let that flow over into your marriage relationship.

Malachi 2:15 has a beautiful phrase, "Guard yourself in your spirit," which describes how we can avoid sin. Once I went to a movie and a few days later got a letter from someone who had gone to see it at the same time and had walked out. He had seen me there, and I didn't walk out; he wanted to know why. For the answer I had to sit down and search my own heart. I came up with two or three pages, a yellow legal pad long, about it.

Some people can handle certain things that others can't. I look at a glass of wine, and it doesn't bother me in the least. People severely addicted to alcohol can't even look at one. I can look at a plate of food, and if I decide that's too much, or I don't want to eat that kind, I'll say no to it. Other people can't. Things that inflame some people so that they lose control don't bother others at all.

What do we do in response to such situations? We guard ourselves in the Spirit. We have to know before God what we can handle and what we can't, and we have to discipline ourselves. That's preventive.

## Remedial medicine

How about remedial medicine? Jesus was confronted in the temple one day by some pious Jews who dragged in a woman caught in adultery. They tested Jesus by saying, "Moses says she should be stoned. What do you say?"

Jesus answered, "Whoever is without sin, throw the first stone." While he waited, her accusers walked out, one by one. The Lord turned to her and said, "You're forgiven. Now go away and don't do it again."

Put all that together and you'll find some beautiful truths in this story, told in John 8. You'll discover a loving Savior who forgives. If anyone guilty of adultery in any form repents of it, confesses, and turns from it, he or she will be forgiven; but that forgiveness cost Christ his life on the cross. It didn't come cheap. The remedial cure requires a repentant spirit, a loving Savior, and a caring community.

What about that caring community? I'll never forget the day we opened our new church building. Ben Haden, minister of First Presbyterian Church in Chattanooga, came to give the first address from our pulpit. He taught from this text: "Do not be deceived: Neither the sexually immoral or idolaters nor adulterers nor male prostitutes nor homosexual offenders nor thieves nor the greedy nor drunkards nor slanderers nor swindlers will inherit the kingdom of God" (1 Cor. 6:9-10).

When I heard that text, I thought, *Ben, what on earth are you doing? You're supposed to be celebrating the opening of a new building!* But when I read the next verse, I realized what he planned to say. "And that is what some of you were. But you were washed, you were sanctified, you were justified in the name of the Lord Jesus Christ and by the Spirit of our God" (verse 11).

Ben went on to tell us that because we had a new building we shouldn't become too smug, because in this building we would gather forgiven sinners. That's what a church is: a community of forgiven sinners. It doesn't condone sin or condemn sinners. The church knows what we're all capable of and preaches the love and grace and forgiveness of Christ. It warmly embraces those who repent of their sins, seek his forgiveness, and live rightly before him.

Finally, those who repent need a forgiving family. If you want to know what it means to forgive those who have engaged in this kind of sin, read the Old Testament book of Hosea. The prophet married a harlot named Gomer. A few years after the wedding, she committed adultery, and Hosea forgave her magnificently. Like Gomer, we too fall away from God. We need Hosea's compassion for others. Always remember that those who are forgiven much—and that's all believers—make great forgivers, because when we look around us, we can say, "There but for the grace of God go I."

1. How does adultery defy God and deny love?

2. How can one kind of unfaithfulness spread to other areas of unfaithfulness?

3. What are four causes of adultery?

4. What preventive measures can protect your marriage against adultery?

5. What role does forgiveness play in preventing further adulterous sin?

# EIGHT

You shall not
steal.

Exodus 20:15

# 8
# Handling Property Properly

Not long ago I had lunch with George Gallup, of the Gallup poll. About a thousand other people were also there, but I had a chance to talk to him after his presentation, and I found out some interesting things about Christians today.

He told me that though religion has grown in popularity in our country, morality has declined. The Gallup organization polled the people of the United States and found out that church attendance has increased, along with Bible reading and other religious behaviors. But when he did a test in conjunction with the *Wall Street Journal,* asking questions about expense accounts, income taxes, and so on, the polling group noticed that a high percentage did not regard cheating on these items as stealing. Even more surprising, this attitude was evident whether or not the people polled went to church. From that George Gallup concluded that many of those who claim an interest in religion do not let it affect their personal concept of morality in behavior.

Like those businessmen, many of us have a desperately inadequate view of what constitutes stealing, and we all need to take a look at what the Bible says on the subject.

The eighth commandment says it succinctly: "You shall not steal." In fact, the original Hebrew really has only two words: "Not steal." That's pretty straightforward.

But what shapes and sizes does stealing come in? Two: stealing from people, and stealing from God.

# Stealing from People

In order to steal from a human being we need not merely take his money. We may deprive him of any number of rights by theft.

## Deprivation of property

You can steal a person's property. Ask a few people what "property" is, and you'll start an interesting discussion, because ideas about it and how you should hold it vary. We all know of the Communist idea that property belongs to the state, and we understand that the capitalist says it belongs to the individual. But how many of us are aware of the biblical teachings on the subject? The Bible clearly disagrees with both these views.

Scripture certainly teaches us that property is necessary and certain things should not be taken from the owner. Some of the ancient laws recorded in Deuteronomy 24 say if you take collateral for a loan from a person, you have to be careful about what you take. You cannot take his millstone, for instance; he needs that to grind his corn and get his flour to make his bread, in order to survive. You can't take his cloak and keep it overnight, because in cold weather he would probably freeze to death without it. He needs it.

What else do we need? First Timothy 6:8 tells us we should feel content with shelter, food, and clothes. Scripture says we have the right to property in terms of those needs, and they should not be taken from us. The tenth commandment, "You shall not covet," provides a list of what we have the right to. But how many of us are satisfied with that list? We'd like to have blanket approval on our ownership of anything we desire. But God doesn't give us that or the kind of exclusive rights we may think we have. The Bible teaches that even the property we do have rights to we hold in trust, and here's where the biblical teaching differs from that of both capitalists and Communists.

Even though we *need* certain things and have a right to them, our ownership is not an absolute right. Psalms 24:1 says, "The earth is the Lord's, and everything in it." Everything in existence belongs to him, and that includes what you own. Your house is the Lord's. The land it sits on belongs to God. The car you drive belongs to him. Everything you have and everything you are is his; he has privileged you with it in trust. When one person steals another's property, he not only takes something that person needs, he also takes something God entrusted to him; therefore the thief has deprived God of it and has sinned against him. In this sense we can't really separate stealing from people and stealing from God.

## Deprivation of liberty

In order to steal, we need not take a person's property. Instead we may deprive him of liberty, his freedom to be or do. Although we most often associate such actions with totalitarian regimes, while rejoicing in the freedom we enjoy in our country, let's not forget that we, too, may deprive a person of the kind of freedom God intended him to have.

What does it mean to take a person's liberty? The Bible gives us a clue in its view of slavery—one very different from ours. Scripture recognizes something significant when it says a slave belongs to the Lord. In other words, a person might own another one, and he might deprive that slave of liberty, but the owner still should remember that the slave belongs to God. Without owning a slave, I, too, could deprive someone else of a freedom God gave him.

In the Old Testament era, when people stole property they didn't pack up a thief and send him to jail (where he could learn new tricks of the trade from other criminals so he wouldn't get caught next time), but they controlled him so that he could work to earn a restitution worth twice, four times, or even five times the value of what he had taken. However, the penalty for stealing a person's liberty was harsh. If a person kidnapped another, stealing that person's God-given freedom, the punishment was death. Stealing another's freedom was a serious offense.

## Deprivation of dignity

Stealing can be depriving another person of dignity. Everyone has a certain reputation and character. If we take someone's reputation and character from him by libeling and smearing him, we have robbed him.

In Acts 19 we can see a rather interesting example of this. Paul went into Ephesus and preached there. He had a remarkable response—many turned away from the worship of the goddess Diana. This hit at the trade of the silversmiths, who made money by selling ugly little silver shrines of Diana. The representative of the Most Honorable Order of Silversmiths of Ephesus, branch department number 217, got upset, and Demetrius the shop steward served up a revolt. A crowd came into the stadium (which you can still see if you visit Ephesus today). Among other things, Demetrius complained, "These men are robbing our goddess of her majesty."

With people we can do that, too. We can take away another's majesty, his dignity, the essence of his personhood. In so doing, we've robbed him of something God invested him with.

We may also deprive a person of his dignity by robbing him of justice. Isaiah 10:1-3 decries this with the words:

Woe to those who make unjust laws, to those who issue oppressive decrees, to deprive the poor of their rights and withhold justice from the oppressed of my people, making widows their prey and robbing the fatherless. What will you do on the day of reckoning, when disaster comes from afar? To whom will you run for help? Where will you leave your riches?

God doesn't paint a pretty picture of the results of this kind of theft, does he?

## Deprivation of opportunity

We may steal from another by depriving him of opportunity. For example, some do not understand that when they steal from their employers they have deprived them of their right to make a profit, so they don't call their acts theft. In saying that they disagree with God; the Bible talks about this in Paul's letter to Titus, when he tells Titus to teach slaves not to steal from their masters.

Now some of us may feel like slaves, but our lives hardly compare unfavorably to those of New Testament slaves. At most you may feel your company doesn't pay enough for what you do, or that they make too much profit, and because of that you may feel comfortable stealing from them. You don't call it "stealing," though.

We've developed many acceptable ways of stealing from employers today. One is calling in sick when you're not. Not only have you lied, you've stolen. But most people regard that as an absolute right. You have so many vacation days and so many sick days. You may think, "Oh, I haven't been sick, but I have the right to these sick days; therefore, I will simply call in sick. I'll take them." In doing this, you rob your employer of his right: a full day's work for a full day's wage.

Maybe you don't call in sick, but you check in late or check out early. Or you take a longer break than you're allowed. Maybe you've taken home pens or notepads that don't belong to you, or you make telephone calls you've not been given the freedom to make.

Or you may deprive someone of opportunity by denying the government its right to govern. The Lord Jesus made a simple, basic statement: "Give to Caesar what is Caesar's, and to God what is God's" (Matt. 22:21), and people have argued about those words ever since.

When you want a great discussion, bring up the subject of government. Talk about taxes. I'll guarantee that everyone who never says a word about the Bible will have a lot to say on the subject. People have definite views on these subjects.

The Bible teaches that you should pay your taxes; you must not cheat on them. If you do, you're stealing from the government.

Recently someone suggested that the best way to get rid of America's deficit would be to get people to pay their back taxes. In no time at all we'd pay off the deficit. Our economic ills reflect our fundamental moral problem. Though we claim to be very upright and religious, we remain guilty of stealing from both our employers and our government.

## Rich and poor

Most often when we think of stealing we think in terms of the "have-nots" taking from the "haves" what is not theirs. In the world we have a dichotomy between the haves and the have-nots. The haves have what the have-nots have not. It's a simple law of economics. The have-nots have not what the haves have.

If you're a have, you'll think it'd be great if it stayed that way. Unfortunately the have-nots won't let it stay that way, because they want what the haves have. So our natural idea of stealing says the have-nots take what the haves have.

The Bible says relatively little about this kind of theft. But it does say a lot about the haves stealing from the have-nots. "What?" you cry. "Stealing is the have-nots ripping off haves. It's mugging; it's shoplifting. It's them doing all kinds of things like this!"

That is stealing, but so is the haves taking from the have-nots. In Deuteronomy 24:14-15 the Bible says if you've got a poor and needy man working for you, you've got him over a barrel, because he really needs the work. He's desperate. You want to keep him over the barrel so that you can get the last drop out of him; therefore, you don't pay him his evening wages. The law of Moses flatly forbade such actions. You had to pay a man at the end of the day; you could not owe it to him.

In other words, the Bible says you steal from others, when you have economic control over them, if you do not give them their due when it is due. In addition Scripture teaches that it is stealing when you look upon suffering people and do nothing about it. When we feel we have the perfect right not to help them, we may have the freedom to feel that way, but we never got it from Scripture.

The Old Testament clearly states that the wealthy have an obligation to the poor. This flies in the face of the thinking of many conservative Christians in the United States of America. But Scripture teaches those who have also have a God-given responsibility to those who have not.

For example, the Old Testament says those who owned fields could not cut the corners of a field during harvest. The law allowed the poor people to come in at the end of the day and reap the corners for themselves.

In addition the harvesters could not glean after they had gone through a field. They could not go over the field at the end and rake up all the bits left in the field; they had to leave that for the poor. The Bible squarely places the responsibility for the poor people with those who have means. It insists that those who denied the needy the opportunity to survive stole from them.

Scripture most clearly describes this in the laws of the Jubilee. In the fiftieth year of a cycle, in the Old Testament times, all property reverted to its original owner. The land in Israel had been apportioned out, and the people understood that the land was the Lord's and the fullness thereof. When they received land, they held it as a trust. They could harvest it, but they had to leave some for the poor.

In land ownership everybody started out on equal footing. But some were smarter than others, and some worked harder than the rest. Others were stupid and lazy. In no time flat some had more, while others had less.

In a time of calamity the wealthy might cash in on others' misfortune. As time went on the rich got richer, and the poor got poorer. God had something to say about that situation. On the fiftieth year, according to his law, all the property reverted to the original owner, which limited how rich the rich could get and how poor the poor could become. The rich had an ongoing responsibility for the poor.

When we look at this in a scriptural light, we discover that stealing means a lot more than mugging or shoplifting. Whoever would have thought that in our sophisticated society we'd have to see signs on fashionable boutique walls reminding us that shoplifting is stealing? We should know that. But for some reason we don't want to hear about it.

# Stealing from God

It may surprise you that we can steal from God—and that we can do it in two ways.

## Contradictory behavior

First, we can rob God of his credibility by our inconsistent behavior.

Remember when the Lord Jesus went into the temple, made a whip, drove the people out, turned the tables over, and created chaos? Among other things, that day he said, "How dare you turn this house of prayer into a den of robbers?" So some folks have said, "There you are. If you do business on church premises, you're making it into a den of robbers." When we proposed opening a bookstore at my church, I got a number of letters from people saying, "If you open that bookstore at Elmbrook Church, we will leave the church. How dare you make a house of prayer into a den of robbers?"

With all due respect to these people, I don't think they adequately understood the meaning of that story. Jesus did not mean you should never do business on the church grounds.

He wanted to get across a principle the people there had missed. When they sold all the animals for sacrifice in the temple, some terribly dishonest behavior took place right before everyone's eyes. They charged outrageous prices, and anyone who brought his own animal had to exchange it for one in the temple—and had to pay even more money for an animal of equal value. The men who did this professed to be spiritual, but their behavior was not. It wasn't a very good example of God's ways of doing things.

Today some people within the church come to us and say quite openly that they live together outside of matrimony. They're having sexual relations outside marriage and see no reason why they should stop. In doing this, they've made a house of prayer into a den of robbers, because they've robbed God of his credibility. If non-Christians come into a place of worship and see them living like that yet professing to be followers of Christ, the newcomers will say to themselves, "These people are phonies. This whole religion thing is a fake. Forget God."

The best way I know of to rob God of credibility is to loudly profess one thing and live another.

## Tithes and offerings

The second way we can rob God is, as Malachi puts it, by refusing to pay the tithes and offerings. When Malachi talked to the Jews, they resisted him. They argued at every point. Finally he said, "Will a man rob God?"

They asked, "How can we rob God?"

"By refusing to pay your tithes and your offerings," he told them. (See Mal. 3:7-8.)

Have you heard the story of the old ladies who had a new preacher in their church? The first week he preached against drinking, and they came up to him after the service and said, "That's preaching, preacher!"

The second week he spoke against running around with women. They came up to him and encouraged him, "That's preaching, preacher!"

The third week he preached against smoking, and after the message they told him, "That's preaching, preacher."

The fourth week he preached about tithes and offerings. The two women cornered him and complained, "Now you've quit preaching and taken to meddling!"

Some of you will think I've taken to meddling now, because as a pastor and teacher of the Word of God, I must say that some of us rob God. The Old Testament teaches that if the people failed to bring their tithes and offerings to the Lord, they robbed him.

What do we mean by a tithe? Some people have never heard of tithing, and others will say it's giving God 10 percent of your salary. But the 10-percent people have trouble deciding if that's before or after taxes.

What does the Bible teach? According to Deuteronomy 14, the people should give an annual tithe of 10 percent of all they produced to the Lord. In addition the people were to give a wide variety of offerings and sacrifices, and they also brought special thank offerings and special offerings for the building of a temple or tabernacle.

In the church we have a rare breed of people who really get into tithing, but it's not too many of us. Tithers think tithing means giving 10 percent of their income, not more. Yes, God makes that the base, but if we don't want to rob him, we also need to learn that we hold everything in trust for him. We need to get into all kinds of offerings: thank offerings, special offerings, peace offerings. That will take up a substantial part of our incomes.

Right now I can hear someone saying, "We are not under law; we are under grace. That means we don't have to operate on that basis." I'd respond, "You are absolutely right. But wherever did you get the idea that when we come under grace we do less than they had to do under law? Under grace you are so full of gratitude that you take every opportunity to express it, rather than coming under a legalistic attitude that says you only have to give 10 percent."

I visited a church in Florida, where the congregation had just built a new auditorium that cost $5 or $6 million. With great glee the people told me they had moved in debt free; they had paid for it in cash before they opened the doors.

When I asked how they had done it, they told me, "Part of our membership requirement is that people tithe." Then they took me outside and showed me a three- or four-story, $11 million educational wing they had begun to build. Again they told me they'd paid cash for it. How did they do it? By tithing.

Now don't tithe just with the goal of meeting your church's budget, because budgets don't really mean that much. Tithing has a deeper purpose; it means you give to God, you don't rob from him. When you give to God, you honor him. You say, "Hey, God, all my money is in trust from you anyway, and I give it back to you with a glad heart." Through our giving we show we're on his side and that we have compassion for the things and people he has compassion for. We prove our love for him by giving of ourselves.

What if we don't give our tithes and keep what belongs to him for ourselves? That may result from an attitude of first-rate stinginess, or maybe it comes from second-rate sacrifice. Malachi told his people, "Some of you are bringing your offerings to the Lord, and you've got to bring a lamb. So you go through the flock and find one that's lame or blind, and you bring that. Do that to the governor, and see what he'd say! You wouldn't dare do it to him, but you don't mind doing it to God."

Strange, people feel very comfortable with first-rate stinginess and second-rate sacrifice when it comes to God. Why? Because they lack reality of the knowledge of God in their lives.

We also feel comfortable with third-rate motives. See how it works in the story of Ananias and Sapphira, recorded in Acts 5. This couple sold their land and wanted the money, but they wanted the glory, too. In the end it cost them their lives. A high price tag, wasn't it?

What would happen in our churches if we took tithing really seriously and brought along all the offerings, out of our glad hearts? We probably wouldn't even have to worry about budgets anymore. Our churches would need to hire someone just to take care of the finances and channel them into all the worthwhile projects they could find. We'd also have to find new ways to handle the blessings God would pour out into our lives.

You know why? Because God speaks through Malachi and tells us, "If you will bring the whole tithe into the storehouse, you will be able to prove me. Get down to honoring me, and I'll show you what I can do. And I will open the windows of heaven and pour out such a blessing you won't be able to handle it" (see Mal. 3:10). If we do that, we get the blessing; if we don't do it, we may be robbing God.

# Dangers and Damages of Stealing

Various things may happen to those who engage in stealing. You don't have to look far to discover its effects, none of them beneficial!

1. Stealing can lead you into trouble with the law.

2. Stealing will ruin your relationships with others.

3. Theft leads to deception and lies. You'd be hard put to find a thief who doesn't also lie. When someone finds out and confronts him with his actions, he will cover up. When I had a job as a bank examiner, I became very suspicious about one man who had not said or done anything to make me think that way. At the bank they reported him as one of their best employees. In fact, he never took a vacation. As soon as I heard that, I thought, *Uh-oh, a banker who won't take a vacation?* We started to look carefully at the situation and found he wouldn't take a vacation because he wouldn't trust anyone else with his responsibilities. After a month of work on the case, we discovered why. He had one set of books available for the inspectors, when they came in, and another for the customers, when they asked about their accounts. In between those figures lay thousands and thousands of embezzled dollars. The man lied through his teeth for months, denying he had done it, until we categorically proved his theft. When he knew he could no longer get away with his lies, he threw himself under a train.

4. Stealing shrivels the one who does it. His actions run counter to God's law, so they harm him morally and emotionally.

5. Stealing places extra burdens on others. When people shoplift, the companies they steal from do not bear the cost of the lost goods; they simply pass it on to the

consumer. We pay more for our goods because we finance the thieves.

6. Stealing hinders the work of God. When Christians refuse to give to God's work generously and joyously, making it possible for the work to go on, they slow down or halt his work.

## Steal No Longer

Finally, let's take a look at the blessings and bounties that accrue to us when we stop stealing. Ephesians 4:28 tells us, "He who has been stealing must steal no longer." Could anything be clearer? The whole verse reads, "He who has been stealing must steal no longer, but must work, doing something useful with his own hands, that he may have something to share with those in need."

Put all that together and you have a marvelous principle of Christian economics. If you've been stealing, come to repentance. That means admitting to God what you've done and making restitution—giving back or paying back the one from whom you've stolen. We desperately need restitution in our penal system today.

How can it work? W. P. Nicholson, an old Irish evangelist, preached in Belfast when that city was the major shipbuilding capital of the world. The men from the shipyards would put down their tools when the hooter sounded; they would form up and march out of the shipyards, through the streets, to the church where the dynamic speaker preached. They went straight from their tasks, in their work clothes, and filled the church. Then W. P. Nicholson would preach to them powerfully, spreading conviction, insisting on repentance and restitution.

Many men accepted Christ and started to bring back everything they had stolen from the yards. In the end the authorities had to make a public announcement: "Will all those men attending the meetings of Mr. W. P. Nicholson please stop returning stolen goods. We have nowhere to store them." Imagine the unbelievable volume of stolen property that implies. Imagine the blessings!

## The Blessing of Work

We need the joy of hard work, too. One of the Greek words for "work" is allied to the word for "weariness." You can get weary not doing much, but you feel somehow noble about a weariness that comes from hard work, because in the end you know you've produced something. That's what we're here for. Why? The Bible does not promise us the "good life," financially. Instead it says we should produce in order to put ourselves in the position of engaging in the blessing of giving. We need to steal no more in order to give to him that is in need.

When we come to this point we have the blessing of becoming blessings to others. In the name of Jesus we can reach out and add to his credibility—all because we've acted on this premise: "You shall not steal!"

1. Describe four ways, some of them subtle, that we can steal from other people.

2. How does our contradictory behavior become a way of stealing from God?

3. Are you satisfied with your current levels of tithing and giving?

4. What are the dangers and damages of stealing?

5. When is hard work actually a blessing?

# NINE

You shall not
give false testimony
against your neighbor.

Exodus 20:16

# 9
# Speaking the Truth

Remember the concern God felt for his people as he told them they needed to live rightly before him and among one another? In order to guide them, he gave them those ten instructions that would show them how to love the Lord their God with all their hearts and minds and souls and strength and how to love their neighbors as themselves. The ninth commandment would help them show love for their neighbors.

The commandment takes the form of a positive concern expressed in a negative term, to catch people's attention. The flat forbidding of giving false testimony against your neighbor expresses God's desire for his people to love the truth, examine the truth, and live in truth and righteousness. Although we might think of this verse in terms of testimony given in a court of law, other passages of Scripture make it quite clear God by no means limits it to that. It's a good thing! We recognize this in our own judicial system, which says that witnesses must tell the truth, the whole truth, and nothing but the truth. We glibly repeat that phrase, but how much does it mean to us?

Look at any newspaper, and you'll find examples of our real attitudes. Edwin Moses, the great Olympic hurdler and track star, shocked the world when, not long after the 1984 games, he was charged with soliciting an undercover policewoman posing as a prostitute. The case came to court. "I didn't do it," Edwin Moses said. "He did it," the policewoman said.

In another famous trial, William Westmoreland stated that CBS libeled him when they accused him of conspiracy at the highest level of military intelligence. Their program "60 Minutes" reported that he fudged on the numbers for political reasons. He insisted that he didn't. Who was right?

These cases make us wonder. How can we know when someone tells the truth and when he lies? Even if these men did tell the truth, we've seen many other people lie and get away with it. While the court system does its best, it can't guarantee that it always makes the right decision. We've made their job harder by condoning lies by our careless attitude toward the truth.

Today our society is in a state where people at both the highest and lowest levels seem perfectly happy saying anything they want to say; and other people let them. Truth became an early casualty. Lying has turned into a way of life. In fact some circles almost encourage it, giving the impression that you just can't survive without some deception, and you most certainly can't get ahead unless you do it.

Against that background let's hear the Word of God, which says you must not give false testimony against a neighbor. Proverbs 6:16-19 declares, "There are six things the LORD hates, seven that are detestable to him: haughty eyes, a lying tongue, hands that shed innocent blood, a heart that devises wicked schemes, feet that are quick to rush into evil, a false witness who pours out lies and a man who stirs up dissension among brothers." Out of those seven things, notice that two have to do with being a stranger to the truth.

Now we may dress up lying in a lot of ways. We can talk about it, we can excuse it, we can philosophize about it. I've spent some time reading what philosophers say about this, and it's amazing how they can muddy the waters on this subject. It doesn't take much to cover up the truth. Once Winston Churchill did not want to accuse someone of lying in the House of Parliament—that would have been a terrible thing to do. He simply avoided it by accusing that person of "perpetrating a terminological inexactitude." He actually meant, "You're a liar."

Why does lying seem so important to God? Why do people lie? How can we avoid it?

# Why God Prohibits Lying

## Lying and Satan

In John 8:43-45 John records some very powerful and scathing comments the Lord Jesus made to some very religious people. Among other things, he told them,

> Why is my language not clear to you? Because you are unable to hear what I say. You belong to your father, the devil, and you want to carry out your father's desire. He was a murderer from the beginning, not holding to the truth, for there is no truth in him. When he lies, he speaks his native language, for he is a liar and the father of lies. Yet because I tell the truth, you do not believe me!

Jesus' statement immediately put the dangerous business of lying into perspective. He said that when we lie, we are speaking the devil's native language! Satan doesn't know the truth, and Jesus says he reproduces people who do not know the truth—lying becomes their native language, too.

Involving yourself in lying means connecting yourself to the devil. Jesus came to speak the truth, but people involved with the devil cannot even recognize it. So his words outline a massive cosmic struggle between the Father of righteousness and the father of lies. The whole universe—and all the men and women in it—are swept up into the conflict.

Quite naturally from this we begin to understand the struggle between good and evil. The Bible says in Genesis 1 that God made everything and promptly evaluated it. He said, "It's good."

Then you read in John 10 that Jesus came into the world that we might have life and have it to the full. "If God made everything so good," you may feel tempted to ask, "why did Jesus need to come give us more abundant life?" The answer is that another factor came into being. John 10:10 says that the thief had come, intent on killing and stealing and destroying.

As God builds up what is good, Satan intently moves to destroy that good by bringing lies and untruth into areas of truth and reality. That's why God so adamantly opposes lying and so totally supports truth: He recognizes the struggle between himself and the devil, between good and evil, and knows that as people get swept into lies they become strangers to the truth.

A struggle also exists between truth and delusion. In 2 Corinthians 4:4 the apostle Paul refers to the devil as "the god of this age." Paul goes on to say he "has blinded the minds of unbelievers, so that they cannot see the light of the gospel of the glory of Christ." Further on he says, in contrast, "God, who said, 'Let light shine out of darkness,' made his light shine in our hearts to give us the light of knowledge of the glory of God in the face of Christ" (verse 6).

Notice the dichotomy here. Some people have minds so blinded to truth that they live a delusion. But God longs to shine into their darkness as surely as at the creation. He bade the light to shine and banish physical darkness. Some people live in spiritual darkness and delusion; others have their eyes opened to spiritual truth.

## Lying and righteousness

Righteousness struggles against sin, too. God is committed to truth, to right (the Bible calls it righteousness). Sin and evil oppose him. In our own lives we can identify when we get caught up in lying in any form. We also need to understand that we've been caught between righteousness and sin in making that choice.

Can you understand why God takes lying so seriously?

# Why People Lie

Please have three propensities in lying, three ways of lying:

They may lie to themselves.
They may lie to God.
They may lie to their neighbors.

## People lie to themselves

One unique thing about being human is that you can be self-conscious or aware of yourself. In saying this, I don't mean you stand there, blushing sweetly and saying, "Aw, shucks, you know, pardon me for being here. I feel so awkward."

Rather, I mean you have an awareness of yourself and your actions. When I visited Kenya, I went to a game park that spreads over hundreds of square miles. In that park they have a small group of very rare white rhinoceroses—only about five of these precious animals. Because hunters prize the horns of these practically extinct animals and try to kill them, every night the game wardens lock up the rhinos, even though all the other animals range freely over the park. The men even set an armed guard over the beasts.

As we drove through the park, we decided to stop and get a look at the white rhinos. A guard came up and asked if we would like to see them. So we said, "Thank you very much. We'd like to see them—from the car."

"Oh, come out and get a closer look at them," the man invited. So we did. We walked right up to these great big things. They were as big as tanks, and they were munching on a snack of vegetation. One of the guards patted one, and dust and gook came off on his hand.

"Why don't you pat it?" he asked me. I did.

Then the guard went round to the rear end, braced himself against the rhino's feet, got a hold on the tail, and pulled it. "Now you do it," he instructed. So I did.

Suddenly a little voice said to me, Stuart, that is a rhinoceros. You're pulling the tail of a rhinoceros. What are you doing? The voice was mine. I was talking to myself. That's self-consciousness.

Part of me was conscious of me. One part of me pulled the tail of the beast. The other part said, "You're either one of the most courageous people around, or you're the biggest dummy in the area." Got the picture?

If you can talk to yourself about yourself, you're self-conscious. You talk about yourself because you think about yourself. Romans 12:3 tells us we should not think about ourselves more highly than we ought to, but we should think of ourselves soberly. In other words, we should use our God-given consciousness according to the truth.

If we think more highly than we ought—or more "lowly"—we lie to ourselves. We communicate untruth to ourselves. This self delusion is the first step on the pathway to insanity. Some people delude themselves so thoroughly that they no longer know the difference between up and down, black and white, or right and wrong—or reality and unreality.

When we lie to ourselves, we not infrequently perpetrate a crime against ourselves. For instance, I may find myself in a situation, and I look at it. Somebody else talks to me about it and says, "Stuart, you are doing something quite wrong here." In response I immediately come up with all kinds of excuses and rationalizations. I perfectly convince myself the other guy's wrong and I'm right. When I do that, I could be lying to myself.

We pastors often see this in marriage counseling. A couple on the brink of divorce will tell two versions of their troubled story. The counselor must evaluate what's going on in the marriage. As we listen to both parties, it seems that someone has to be lying; both can't be telling the truth.

But often the person hasn't intentionally lied. He (or she) really believes the lies. The two stories don't agree because he's lied to himself and isn't confronting reality. The temptation is for each to blame the troubles on somebody else. The root of much of our lying to ourselves lies in our distaste for the harshness of the reality of our own sin.

## People lie to God

To some, humans lying to God may sound unthinkable. He knows everything. How can we possibly lie to him?

Acts 5 tells a story of the early church. Some people had great need, and others had property. The property owners sold it, brought the proceeds, and put them in the common bank so everyone could be cared for.

One man who did this was named Joseph, a landowner from Cyprus. He was so well liked and well known that the apostles gave him a new name. They called him Barnabas, which means "the son of encouragement." Two other people named Ananias and Sapphira watched Barnabas and thought, "We'd like to do something like that. That kind of recognition would feel good. We've got some land; we'll sell it. Then we can bring the proceeds—not all of them, just some of them—and we can pretend we gave it all."

Ananias and Sapphira did just that, but Peter saw through their deception. He told them, "While the property was yours, it was yours. When you sold the property and got the cash, the cash belonged to you. When you decided to give some to the church, fine. When you decided to give some to the church and pretend you gave it all, that was lying." The important thing they had to realize was, "You weren't lying to men, you were lying to God."

What led Ananias and Sapphira to lie to God? On the one hand they wanted to appear in favor with God, to look good to God's people. But to do things God's way would cost them, challenge them, would require decisions and change. They didn't want the more difficult aspects of serving God. So they tried to capitalize on all the benefits without paying the price. When we pretend to honor God and love him, but won't really do it his way because it would cost us too much, we not only lie to those around us, we also fundamentally communicate untruth to God—we lie to him.

It's bad enough to lie to yourself and create a delusion about yourself; just imagine lying to God about yourself and ending up in a realm of spiritual delusion—a Never-never Land that doesn't reflect the real state of your faith. Christians find it all too easy to fall into this disastrous trap. Maybe you go to church on a Sunday and sing a powerful hymn about serving God, but if you're not careful, and if you don't mean what you sing, you could find yourself very sweetly lying to God the whole time.

Singing a hymn you don't mean may not be a major crime, but it might signal the development of a mindset so far removed from the reality of your heart that you will lie to both yourself and God.

## People lie to other people

Finally, people tend to lie to their neighbors—and they do it in four ways. *The destructive lie* is born of malicious intent and made up of entirely erroneous content.

For example, the Sanhedrin decided Jesus was guilty and wanted the death penalty for him, but they could not prove his guilt. Having decided that he would die even before the trial, they got false witnesses to give evidence. They showed no interest in truth or righteousness. They decided on their goal—to destroy this man. They'd do whatever it took to accomplish that, including lying.

Not uncommonly we find such malice in our own hearts— a desire to destroy, hurt, or hinder someone. If we're not careful, we can go to extremes out of that evil intent, and head toward the goal of destruction.

Jacob's son Joseph, who was sold into slavery, ended up working in the house of Potiphar in Egypt. When Potiphar went away on business, Mrs. Potiphar made eyes at Joseph. And when the young man wouldn't allow her to seduce him, she framed him. She felt so angry and hurt that she wanted to get even with him. She went after him, and he ended up rotting in jail, falsely accused.

The destructive lie is not uncommon when people feel hurt and when they decide to get even. We come across it all too often in today's society.

Next, people employ *the defensive lie*. Peter used this after he made a great profession to the Lord Jesus, "Even if everyone else forsakes you, I will not."

Jesus said, "Oh, yes, you will."

"No, no, I won't. They might; I won't."

Jesus warned him, "Before the cock crows, you will deny me three times."

"Come on," Peter told him. "You don't know what you're talking about." Then he followed Jesus at a distance. (When we start to follow God at any distance, it's always a sign of trouble.)

Eventually Peter was waiting in the courtyard of the place where Jesus was being tried, and a little girl came up to him and said, "I've seen you somewhere before."

"No, you haven't."

"Say that again."

"No, you haven't."

"Hey, that's a Galilean accent!"

"Oh, no, it's not."

"I could have sworn it was."

"No, no, no. You're mistaken."

"I think you're one of his disciples."

"I am not." Then Peter burst into oaths and curses, which means he began to call on God to witness that he was not one of Christ's disciples. Lies, lies, lies, all over the place. Why? Defensive lies. Peter was caught and afraid of exposure, so he tried to get out of the situation by lying about it. All he managed to do was compound his culpability and increase his guilt.

Many years ago an up-and-coming young politician in the British government, who was married to a glamorous actress, was charged with having an affair with a call girl—not just any call girl, but one also having an affair with one of the top people at the Russian embassy. The British legislator was challenged with it in front of the House of Parliament, where he categorically denied it. He lied. The next day it was proven, and the government dismissed him. That man never returned to political life. Everyone said that if he had admitted his wrongdoing, he could have received forgiveness. By denying it, he unnecessarily ended his career. One defensive lie destroyed him.

The *defective lie* is the lie of carelessness, boastfulness, silence, or half-truth. I involve myself in the careless lie when, because of a certain situation, I rather eagerly pass on information not particularly favorable to someone. I don't particularly like that person and feel more than happy to pass on the story about him. I don't bother to check it out, I just gossip about it, and out of sheer carelessness I get myself in the lying business.

Or maybe I lie out of boastfulness. Because I have a fragile ego that needs building up, I make myself out to be something I'm not. I stretch the truth, I exaggerate. I manipulate the truth so I look good.

How about *lies of half-truth?* As a teenager I had a girlfriend long before my parents would permit it. She was also four years older than me. Because of these facts, I didn't dare tell them. When I went out in the evening, I had to explain exactly where I planned to go. I belonged to a nearby boys' club, so I said I was going there—which was true. I went to the club, walked in the front door—"Hey, hey, good to see you"—made sure everybody saw me, and darted straight out the back door. Later I came in through the back door, said "Hey, how you doing? Good to see you," and went out the front door and home.

"Where have you been, Stuart?"

"Boys' club."

"Good."

Where had I been? Well, it was technically half true, but my intent was total deception—lying.

Now we can shrug our shoulders and say, "What is truth? It's all relative. What exactly do you mean by *lie?*" We could read philosophy to find out what other people consider lying. We can discuss it. But I guess it's like what the Supreme Court Judge said about pornography, "I may not be able to define it, but I know it when I see it." You may argue about a lie, but deep down in your heart you'll know when you've done it. Instead of discussing it, face up to the fact that lying gets us into this cosmic struggle, and that's why God opposes it.

It seems so easy to fall into lying. How can we cure this rampant problem?

## The Cure for Lying

How can we combat lying? We need to take advantage of the Christian's provision for avoiding it:

So I tell you this, and insist on it in the Lord, that you must no longer live as the Gentiles do, in the futility of their thinking. They are darkened in their understanding and separated from the life of God because of the ignorance that is in them due to the hardening of their hearts.

Having lost all sensitivity, they have given themselves over to sensuality so as to indulge in every kind of impurity, with a continual lust for more.

You, however, did not come to know Christ that way. Surely you heard of him and were taught in him in accordance with the truth that is in Jesus. You were taught, with regard to your former way of life, to put off your old self, which is being corrupted by its deceitful desires; to be made new in the attitude of your minds; and to put on the new self, created to be like God in true righteousness and holiness.

Therefore each of you must put off falsehood and speak truthfully to his neighbor, for we are all members of one body.

Ephesians 4:17-25

This passage describes three things that come our way: learning the truth, loving the truth, and living the truth. In verse 21, "Surely you heard of him [Christ] and were taught in him in accordance with the truth that is in Jesus," we see a marked contrast to the lying and deception that go on in our world. Jesus is the truth about man, and he stands tall and true.

We may close our eyes to him; we can choose to give lip service to him, yet have no fundamental interest in him. Paul says, "You have learned the truth as it is in Jesus." Have you? Have you decided that truth is found in him, and that which is contrary to him is by definition error? That's a monumental step to achieve.

If you take that step, you will discover the degree to which untruth and deception have become part and parcel of your life. As you begin to recognize the truth in Jesus, you then must reject the lies—the opposition to him.

In the little town in England where I was born, we had iron and ore mines. The workers stacked up all the waste from the mines in slag banks, like mountains. Many of the little houses perched right at the bottom of the slag banks very rarely saw the light of day. The story goes that once a little lady did her laundry and hung it out in the evening. As she hung it out against the black slag banks, she felt all thrilled about how lily white it looked. She forgot the laundry, and overnight it snowed. When she went out the next morning she could not believe how yellow the laundry looked, yet it hadn't changed at all. When you hang your laundry against a black slag heap, it looks fantastic; against a white snow bank, it looks dreadful. Too much of a comparison!

Likewise, if I compare myself to my inside-out, upside-down society, when it comes to truth and illusion, I could look lily white. I really need to put myself against Jesus, who is the truth, and see the truth about God, humankind, and life. When I see the lies, deception, and untruth in my motives and desires, I can come to repentance. I need to receive the living Lord Jesus, who died so that my sins might be forgiven and rose again that he might impart a new power and a dynamic truth to me. The proof of the change that takes place in my heart shows in my new resolve to live in truth and righteousness.

Have you learned the truth in Jesus? Has your life taken a radical turn? Have you found yourself first confronting him, then yielding and responding to him?

When we learn God's truth, we start to love it. Ephesians 4:15 describes the Christian as one who speaks the truth in love. Some people try to hide the truth—and call it love. Others are so truthful they'll destroy you with "truthfulness," and they call that love. Really speaking the truth in love requires a fine balance, which comes when I begin to understand how unloving it is to deceive maliciously, to delude, to destroy or defame someone. I wouldn't want to do that; I want to build others up instead of knocking them down. I begin to love truth and hate lies.

I love truth because it is antisocial to lie. As Norman Geisler says, "Lying undermines the truth that holds mankind together." Our society requires a certain element of trust. We couldn't operate without it. If we didn't have it, imagine the financial system, the credit system! Imagine our legal system. Yet we hedge these things with rules and laws and regulations and commissions and watchdogs, and all kinds of stuff. Why? Because we know at heart we're liars.

Just imagine what would happen if all the rules, laws, and watchdogs, and the free press and politicians were allowed to do exactly what they wanted. Scrap anything else; it's a free-for-all, and everybody can lie. After all, if you reserve the right to lie, why shouldn't everyone else have that right, too?

Take away all the restrictions and safeguards, and what would we have? A society that collapses. Because if everyone has the freedom to lie, there'll be no truth about which to lie. It's antisocial to lie; it's unloving to lie; it's also counterproductive to lie.

Ephesians 4:29, 31 tells us:

> Do not let any unwholesome talk come out of your mouths, but only what is helpful for building others up according to their needs, that it may benefit those who listen. . . . Get rid of all bitterness, rage and anger, brawling and slander, along with every form of malice.

When you get into malice, slander, anger, rage, and bitterness, you destroy yourself! Lying is counterproductive, so we love the truth. Lying also opposes the Spirit. Verse 30 directs us, "And do not grieve the Holy Spirit." The Holy Spirit has another name, the Spirit of Truth, and anything opposed to him in my life deeply grieves him.

When I begin to live the truth, by exhibiting a lifestyle that has honesty and integrity, people begin to recognize it. This is never easy. Make claims to honesty, make claims to integrity, and you set yourself up to be shot at. Remember when Jimmy Carter said, "I won't lie to you"? A correspondent on the White House staff told me that as soon as the president said that, a whole group of correspondents determined to prove that he lied. They weren't interested in anything else.

It's easy to fit right into the crowd, but if you begin to say, "I stand for Christ; I stand for the truth," people will start gunning for you. But take heart, because the Bible says, "Blessed are those who are persecuted because of righteousness." Today we desperately need men and women who will begin to live the truth. When we live the truth, we can begin to talk it. Once we have shown it in our actions, we can start to proclaim it with a degree of credibility. You'd be hard put to sound convincing if you tried to communicate the truth in Jesus and everybody had already proved you a liar. Who would listen to you?

The ninth commandment says some powerful things to us in those few words, "You shall not give false testimony against your neighbor." The New Testament puts the same principle positively when it tells us,

Therefore each of you must put off falsehood and speak truthfully to his neighbor, for we are all members of one body. . . . Do not let any unwholesome talk come out of your mouths, but only what is helpful for building others up according to their needs, that it may benefit those who listen. And do not grieve the Holy Spirit of God. . . . Get rid of all bitterness, rage and anger, brawling and slander, along with every form of malice. Be kind and compassionate to one another, forgiving each other, just as in Christ God forgave you.

Ephesians 4:25, 29-32

We need to discover those truths for ourselves daily, turning from the lies that bind us, to new freedom in Christ.

1. How is lying "speaking the devil's language"?

2. What is the danger of lying to yourself?

3. How can a person lie to God, who is omniscient?

4. What four types of lies do we employ as we lie to our neighbor?

5. Based on Ephesians 4:17-32, what is God's provision for avoiding lying?

# TEN

You shall not covet
your neighbor's house.
You shall not covet
your neighbor's wife,
or his manservant or maidservant,
his ox or donkey,
or anything that belongs to
your neighbor.

Exodus 20:17

# 10
# Forbidden Fruit

This last commandment offers something different from the rest, because while the first nine deal with actions, the last addresses our attitudes. Accordingly, we find it much easier to talk about the first ones, because we don't have a hard time identifying actions. We can see and verify them, while an attitude may easily remain hidden.

Why would God spend all that time on action rules, then suddenly throw in one on attitudes? To a real extent covetousness pervades and prevails in many of the first nine forbidden activities. This last commandment ties in all of them when it talks about how the law relates to what lies inside our hearts.

## Where Does the Commandment Come From?

The word the Hebrews got *covetousness* from has the same root as the word meaning "desire" or "delight." If you think about it a little, you'll latch on to the link between the two ideas. Seeing covetousness as an inordinate desire for something that may very well be delightful makes a lot of sense. After all, who would covet something that held no attraction at all for him? He sees it, likes it, and begins to tell himself he has to have it—he covets.

The command does not imply that we should have no desires and delight in nothing. God initially gave us the desires and filled the world with delightful things for us to enjoy. Having given them, however, he warns us, "Now don't desire delightful things wrongly." That statement clearly confronts us with the problems of identifying those wrong desires and admitting to ourselves how we have mishandled delightful things. We need to find the right balance, because along with giving us the desires and delightful things, God has also denied us certain things. If we ignore what God has set off limits, simply allowing our desires to go unfettered, we find ourselves deep in covetousness.

## God-Given Desires

God has given us a number of good desires that we may pervert from his purpose by our attitudes. First, he has clearly given us the desire to acquire. In itself nothing is wrong with that. He gave squirrels a desire to hoard nuts in the fall, and it's a good thing he did, because otherwise they would never survive winter. He gave birds a desire to collect straw, mud, and feathers to build a nest; and if he hadn't, they wouldn't have a place to lay their eggs and raise their progeny. By the same token he gives us a basic desire to acquire things. Our God-given survival instincts are clearly related to this acquisitiveness.

God also gives us the desire to succeed. We can see the influence that has on us in the common fear of failing. If we didn't feel so afraid, we would attempt to do more than we do. But we try to avoid the downer of failure because we have a built-in expectation and desire for success. Presumably God

172

put us in this world to achieve something, to be something. We want to do those things, but we see no merit in failing at what he wants. So we avoid anything that might not end in success.

We have a God-given desire to produce. When he created humankind, God made it clear that he expected people to take the raw materials with which he had filled the world and to use them for the glory of God and the benefit of humankind. Anyone who fails to do so lives below his God-given humanity and the desire to progress that he gives. We all should enjoy that tremendous drive to discover more, to bring more and more of the divine creation into subjection in order to derive benefits from it.

## God-Given Things

God has given us delightful things, too. He made the world, put man and woman in it, and they looked around and called it "pleasant." When God saw his creation he said, "That's good." The earth and Adam and Eve were delightful pieces of work. God doesn't make anything shoddy; he filled our world with good things.

Truth is delightful. In Psalm 19:10 the Bible says we should desire his precepts, that God's truth is delightful, more precious than gold, and something about it enraptures our soul. To us he has given the exciting ability to know truth. God has taken the initiative to reveal truth to us, and he says we can find it in his Word. As we work the silver mine of God's Word, enjoying a delightful exploring process rather than being confused about life, we find ourselves locked into the truth.

The apostle Paul says we should desire (or, in the old translations, covet) gifts because God has given us delightful, desirable gifts. He has filled our lives with them. Of course Paul speaks specifically about spiritual gifts (see 1 Cor. 12; 14), but God has also given us much more.

So you put this all together, and what conclusion do you come to? That God has filled creation with love and truth and all manner of delightful gifts. In addition, he has given us desires.

Covetousness means our God-given desires have gone wrong. We may simply describe it as greed, and in actual fact some desires may easily move into greed. Or we may call it lusting after beautiful things, but that ignores the fact that God made them beautiful. We need to think carefully about what we would include here.

God has given us certain denials along with those desires and gifts. He has said, "So far and no farther!" He has told us "This person [or that thing] is off limits." What does he deny us? Let's look at four areas.

## Desiring excessively

God does not prohibit us from desiring, but he does deny us the right to desire excessively. If we do that, we have gotten into covetousness.

But it is difficult to determine what is excessive. If you start working it out, you'll discover one person's excess describes another's normal experience. If we don't think carefully, we may characterize as need what God calls "greed." We have to respond to him with sensitivity. For if we move out of the area of genuine satisfaction into the insistence of naked greed, we tread in forbidden areas.

Read the Old Testament prophets, and you will find that they continually complained to God's people that the covenant people had become consumed by greed. Over and over

God makes it clear that one of the reasons the Hebrews went off into captivity was their covetousness. They desired far more than they needed and thereby demonstrated how covetousness had consumed them.

## Desiring illegitimately

Second, God denies us the right to desire illegitimately, despite the fact that we may see delightful things and want them. For some things God says, "No entry. Keep out. No way. Forbidden territory." He's made it abundantly clear.

In the beginning God put man and woman in the world, demonstrated his love for them, and only wanted their love in return. But you can't make someone love you. You can't grab hold of him by the hair and say, "Fall in love with me." You can only have love when a person makes that free choice. If you can only love by choice, you have to allow the person the ability to choose. So God gave Adam and Eve—and all of us—options. He filled the whole area with delightful things, and in the middle puts a fence around one thing, saying, Don't Touch! If Adam and Eve chose to obey, they would demonstrate their love. If they disobeyed, they would show disdain for God. Maybe the tree God fenced in was no more beautiful than the others. The man and woman certainly had more trees in the garden than they could handle. Only one was forbidden territory, forbidden fruit.

What happened? Of course those two went right ahead, climbed over the fence, grabbed the stuff off that forbidden tree, and demonstrated disdain for God.

God has set up similar limitations on all other areas. On some things he puts up a No Trespassing sign. He moves into certain areas of our lives and says, "This is a delightful thing. You have desires that respond to that thing, but don't touch, because to do that would be illegitimate." We can simply say, "Get lost, Lord!" But if you see a delightful thing God has placed off limits and hold back, you demonstrate your love for him.

When we insist on desiring what is illegitimate, we fall into covetousness and insult God. Joshua 7 clearly illustrates this with the story of Achan. When the children of Israel came into the Promised Land, God forbade them to take plunder. Achan saw some gold and silver and some beautiful clothes and took them. The Israelites went into battle and got roundly defeated. Immediately God told Joshua of the sin in the camp, and they worked by process of elimination until they confronted Achan. What did he confess to when he came forth? Covetousness.

## Desiring exploitatively

If we desire things at the expense of someone else, we exploit that person for our benefit. God speaks against this very powerfully indeed in 2 Peter 2:3: "In their greed these teachers will exploit you with stories they have made up. Their condemnation has long been hanging over them, and their destruction has not been sleeping."

The tenth commandment illustrates what God expects by prohibiting coveting a neighbor's house, wife, maidservant, manservant, his ox or ass, and then God says—in case he hasn't said it clearly enough—nor anything that is your neighbor's. What does that mean? If you see your neighbor's possessions and think he's doing nicely, and you say, "I want what he's got," and you set out to get it, you will exploit him for personal advantage. That is the essence of covetousness.

How easily we do that in our society, which builds so much on competition and the survival of the fittest. How quickly our desires begin to exploit others!

## Desiring exclusively

God also denies us the right to desire exclusively, just to want more and more things. In Luke 12 we read of a time when Jesus spoke to the people, and one of the crowd said, "Teacher, tell my brother to divide the inheritance with me." Jesus replied, "Man, who appointed me a judge or an arbiter between you?" Then he said, "Watch out! Be on your guard against all kinds of greed; a man's life does not consist in the abundance of his possessions." Our society flatly repudiates the Golden Rule and Christ's teachings on this point. Instead it tells us, "We have the inalienable right to pursue happiness," and the clear implication is that we find happiness in possessions. In the original draft of the Declaration of Independence, Thomas Jefferson wrote that man had the inalienable rights of life, liberty, and the pursuit of *possessions*. The committee that worked on the document changed the wording, but our thinking hasn't changed at all. We all feel our happiness lies mostly with our things. Jesus says, "No, it doesn't." We answer, "Yes, it does." Here modern North American society and Jesus meet head to head. "Watch out," says Jesus. "Be on your guard against all kinds of greed, because if you think you have the inalienable right to happiness, and if you link your happiness with your possessions, then to be more happy you will want more possessions, and that's covetousness."

He goes on to illustrate what he means when he talks about a certain rich farmer who did very well, got a bumper crop, and didn't know where to put it all. He would simply expand, he decided; pull down his old barns, which were obsolete anyway, and build bigger, better ones. He thought to himself, "You have done a good job. You have plenty of good things laid up for many years. Now take life easy. Eat, drink, and be merry." That farmer sat back and voted himself a roaring success, but God gave him an *F*. "Fool," he said, "This very night your life will be demanded from you. Then who will get what you have prepared for yourself?" (Luke 12:20). That's what happens to anyone who stores up things for himself, but is not rich toward God.

In writing to Timothy, Paul said we bring nothing into the world, and it is clear we will take nothing out. What do you do between the nothing you start with and the nothing you end with? If you get absorbed with a lot of things, you have simply moved from nothing to things and back to nothing. We need another standard of measurement. Jesus put it this way, "Store up for yourselves treasure in heaven, where moth and rust do not destroy, and where thieves do not break in and steal" (Matt. 6:20).

If I get greedy, caught up with things, what happens to eternal issues? What happens to the spiritual elements of life? If I live with things all my life and forget God, I'll end up a nothing. That's why God denies us the right to desire exclusively.

Remember, he gave us the desires and made the delightful things. But he built in the denials, too. Covetousness means worshiping desire, committing my life to the fulfilling of my wants. I do it when I pursue one delightful thing after another and reserve the right to them without any restrictions.

# What Does Covetousness Do?

Covetousness leads to dishonesty and injustice. David saw Bathsheba. He lusted after her; he coveted her. Clearly he understood the tenth commandment. But she looked delightful. David was all man and had God-given desires. Although he knew God had put her off limits, he denied God's limit and committed adultery. And that was just the beginning. That opened a sad chapter of dishonesty, injustice, and one disaster after another in David's life.

Today, when we go for all the gusto we can get, ignoring God's denial, we open up much hurt and pain in our lives. We can see the results on every hand.

Let's face it, we are constantly confronted with beautiful people, and a lot of us don't have entirely satisfactory marriages. Our ideas are twisted by societal influences about what sex and love should be. If our partners don't measure up to that false standard, we'll focus on the problems and find "delightful" alternatives to them. As we move off into all kinds of exotic ways to enjoy ourselves, we may have fun and excitement, but we may also wreck people's lives. Let's call covetousness what it is: sin that leads to all manner of destruction.

Look at Ahab, Jezebel, and Naboth. Naboth had a little vineyard, a piece of the family territory that God had given him. King Ahab got all the territory around it and wanted that vineyard. He went to Naboth and said, "Hey, listen, I want your vineyard. Just let me have it, and I'll pay you and give you some other territory."

Naboth replied, "I can't do that. This is God-given land that belongs to my family. It's been ours for generations, and it has to stay in the family. Even if you bought it now, it would have to be returned to me at the Jubilee. You understand that, Ahab."

Ahab went away and sulked, but his wife, Jezebel, didn't like her hubby sulking. So she said, "What's the matter?"

"I can't have Naboth's vineyard," the king pouted.

"Don't worry about that. I'll fix it."

She fixed it all right. She lusted after the vineyard and went after it for her husband. Jezebel put Naboth up in the public place and brought forth witnesses against him. They charged him with unspeakable things, and by law they put him to death.

"Great. Go get your vineyard, husband," the queen announced.

Simple covetousness led to injustice, which led to betrayal and murder—all kinds of unspeakable things. In other places the Hebrew word translated "covetousness" means "to cut off." Cut off easily leads to "rip off."

Covetousness also creates insatiable demands. In Mark 7, Jesus described it this way, "Look, Pharisees," he said. "Don't think what you put into your body corrupts it. That's not what does it; it's what comes out of your body that's corrupt." He listed a whole lot of stuff that comes out, including covetousness. "It's there; it's within us," he warned. We all share that built-in, natural tendency to covet.

If we accept that, do we also accept the fact that our society lies in dire danger? One of the Greek words for *covet* means "to have more"—just more and more. In recent years we have worshiped at the shrine of an expanding economy. We want everybody to have a job, and that's a noble goal. If everyone has a job, we'll have increased production. The more we produce, the more we have to sell. If we want to sell more and more things, it means people have to buy more and more. So we work to persuade people to buy more.

How on earth can we do that? Well, some smart business people know the theory of Mark 7, even if they've never read it in the Bible. They know everybody has a tendency toward covetousness. So our expanding economy learns to manipulate the consumer.

Now we've gotten into a vicious circle, because if we cut back, we end up with more and more people out of work. They become more and more of a burden on society, have less and less income, pay less and less in taxes, and we've entered a nasty economic downward spiral. At the root of the whole problem, we have our tendency toward self-interest, which leads us into covetousness, because our society and economic principles almost demand it. Chances are, we don't even realize what's happening.

In his book *Wealth of Nations* Adam Smith, writing in 1776, said, "Man's basic most important motivating force in all economic matters is the drive of self-interest." In other words, "What's in it for me?"

You want something more up-to-date? George F. Will wrote in 1984: "The most familiar and fashionable variety of conservatism is strangely soothing. It tends complaisantly to define the public good as whatever results from the unfettered pursuit of private ends."

He points out the flaw in our thinking when we assume that national good can come out of everybody having the freedom to pursue their own selfish ends. If he's right—and I think our economy proves he is—we're sitting on a powder keg. On the one hand our economy says, "More, more, more. Produce more, sell more, get more." On the other hand God warns us, "Don't covet. Your greed will kill you." Are we sensitive to this weakness in the spirit of our age?

Ephesians 5 tell us the pursuit of personal gain can become an idol. We get so caught up in improving our lot, making our self-interest dominate our lives, that if we're not careful, we worship at the idol of self-interest, in the shrine of personal gain. When that happens, we've confused our moral judgment by our covetousness.

What happened to the man in Luke 18 who wanted eternal life? Jesus told him to get rid of his possessions, come back, and follow him. That young man answered, "No way." The Lord Jesus made it clear that this wealthy fellow deified material things—that was where his heart was. Jesus said, "Where your treasure is, there your heart will be also." If your treasure's here on earth, that's where your heart will be. If your treasure is stored up in heaven, your treasures down here will be relatively insignificant. When we get this wrong, we often don't even realize it.

## How Can We Respond?

When we have it all backwards, we find ourselves worshiping ourselves at the expense of others. All that matters is what we get and what we want, getting what we desire, doing what we want to do, and going where we want to go. What can we do to combat it? First we have to take what God says seriously. When it comes to coveting, he says, "Don't." We need to search our hearts and ask some questions. Am I greedy for position, prestige, praise, or possessions? Is my ego so fragile that I need more and more possessions to make me happy? More praise to make me feel good about myself? Am I hungry for more prestige, greedy to be recognized by more and more people? Do I need a secure position that no one will challenge? Do I constantly reach for these things?

We need to search our hearts, to ask ourselves if self-interest primarily motivates us. Do we use the words *I*, *me*, and *mine* too often? Do we frequently think only of ourselves? Does the world seem to revolve around us?

If we spend much time with such things and little with the Word of God, we probably are riddled with covetousness and don't even realize it. If we see our covetousness, we need to confess that sin, saying, "This is where I moved into forbidden territory." Then we have to adjust our lifestyles. We can easily talk about searching our hearts and confessing sin, but we need to take some action in our lives, too.

What happened in the course of pursuing all those things? Did you do so in order to share them and make them available to others? We may give our tithes, and as we succeed in the things of this world that money grows and grows, but boy, that remaining 90 percent gets bigger too, and we spend it extravagantly.

What does it mean to limit our lifestyles? We look at the way we live and say, "This far and no farther." We do not need that house or the expensive vacation. We do not have to purchase another new car. We avoid status-symbol buying and unnecessary spending. Instead, as God gives us more and more, we discover, to our delight, that we have more and more to give. We have more to share.

We find it hard to call covetousness *sin*, repent, and turn from it. Because they don't exist, I can't offer you any simple solutions. Scripture says, "Godliness with contentment is great gain." All of us want contentment, but we've swallowed the lie that the more we have, the more contented we'll feel. Really, the more we have, the more worried we become about keeping it. The more we have, the more we want.

To cure this, we have to put a lid on it, and we have to see expansion as an opportunity to give as unto the Lord. If I love money, I overlook the fact that the love of money is the root of all evil. I'd better get back to feeling satisfied with food and clothing. Why? Because the writer of Hebrews says we can be content because the Lord is our portion. If we want to live as if we really believed that, we'll have to make some radical changes in our lives.

Will it be worth it?

You can count on it!

1. How does the tenth commandment encompass the commandments that come before?

2. How does a wrong approach to God-given things lead to covetousness?

3. What four ways can our desires, which have been given by God, be exaggerated in covetousness?

4. Give an example of how covetousness can lead to dishonesty and injustice.

5. How does covetousness snowball into insatiable demands?

6. How does our moral judgment become confused because of covetousness?

# 11
# Meeting the Commands' Demands

When God brought his chosen people out of Egypt, he established a covenant with them. He would be their God, and they would be his people. He wanted to work through them in all the nations around them, demonstrating what it meant to have a relationship with him. The Israelites would love the Lord their God with all their heart and mind and soul and strength; they would love their neighbors as themselves. Those actions would show they were his unique people.

To give them practical help in showing God was number one in their lives, he gave them four commandments. To help them know how to love their neighbors, he gave them six more.

## Keeping the Commandments

Today, thousands of years after God first gave those Commandments, to what extent do we have to keep them? How do we meet the demands of the Commandments? What should they mean to us?

## No one righteous

In Romans 3:20, Paul says, "Therefore no one will be declared righteous in his [that is, God's] sight by observing the law; rather, through the law we become conscious of sin." That verse makes two very important statements about the Ten Commandments. First it says that no one will ever be right with God because he or she has fulfilled the Ten Commandments. That comes as a surprise to some people.

You'll come across many folks who will tell you, "I live by the Ten Commandments." They'll say it with a smile of satisfaction on their faces. The fact that they can't even recite the Commandments doesn't bother them at all. They don't know them, but they live by them. "It's my code of ethics, and that's enough," they'll tell you.

Some people, particularly those brought up in areas with a profound religious influence, feel that if you make even a half-hearted attempt at keeping the Commandments, you're okay. God thinks you're a good guy and feels just delighted to have you on his side. But that's wrong thinking. Scripture declares quite categorically, "No one will be declared righteous in God's sight by observing the law." Why? Because no one, except Christ, has ever done it. Paul describes the law this way, "The law is holy, it is righteous, it is good, and it is spiritual." But then he goes on to say, "Those of us who would be justified—declared righteous by fulfilling the law— have got to remember something. We're required to continue in all the law to do it. We are not allowed to approach the Ten Commandments with selective indifference."

Have you noticed how we tend to pick and choose among the Commandments? If we're really into the decline of our society, we notice the one that says, "You shall not commit adultery." We get after all those adulterers around the place and attack those who think adulterous thoughts. We really come down hard on all those sinners!

But the fact that God said, "You shall not covet" rolls off us like water off a duck's back. We figure it's all right to be greedy, as long as we don't commit adultery. Or we feel we can lust after property, wealth, or position, as long as we don't lust after neighbor's spouse.

God doesn't give us the freedom to have such attitudes. If we want to keep the Ten Commandments, we have to keep all of them, and I have yet to meet the person who can go down the whole ten and say that he's kept them all.

One young man who met Jesus thought he had kept them. The Lord Jesus listened with great interest as he told of his perfections. He responded, "Well done, young man. There's only one thing you need to do now. Go away, sell off all your property, and give it away. That's all you need to do. Then come back and be my disciple." When he heard that, the young man gagged on the words and went away sad. Why? Because he approached the Ten Commandments with selective indifference. He wanted to get rid of number ten. It said, "You shall not covet," and he was riddled with covetousness. Jesus put his finger on the spot.

If we want to keep the Commandments, we can never slip up. Sometimes we have spiritual high points, and we feel all enthusiastic. We see a TV program or go to a conference or go to church and get all pumped up. Then we begin to run out of gas. As we leave the meeting or stop watching TV we hear a *hiss-s-s*. Soon we can see the sag it causes in our spiritual lives. If we want the Ten Commandments to justify us, we can't have high points and low points. We can't only feel interest in them spasmodically. We have to keep all ten, externally and internally, all the time.

## Conscious of sin

Romans 3:20 also tells us the second thing we need to learn from the Commandments. "No one will be declared righteous in his sight by observing the law; rather, through the law we become conscious of sin."

Perhaps we feel rather pleased with ourselves in thinking we're rather nice people. Our mothers taught us the social graces, how to behave, and we can cover up certain less-attractive things. We know how to get along with people. Maybe we've even learned how to make friends and influence people. But what are we when we aren't performing? How are we when we're alone? We need to know ourselves as we really are. The Bible says the law helps us do that.

Some time ago, when Jill and I visited the Ivory Coast, we went to a school for missionary children. One day at that school, some children were playing around the base of a tree and found a hole in which they saw something beautiful indeed. They had a wonderful time looking and chattering about it, until one of the teachers noticed what they were up to. He investigated and immediately said, "Kids, get away from that." He herded them off and rushed to get three or four African workers.

One of the men climbed down the hole, while the others held on to him. Then this beautiful thing lying in the hold suddenly struck, grabbed onto the man's leg, and the two workers pulled both man and beautiful beast out and with a machete chopped off the head of the twenty-five-foot-long python. I saw the skin hanging on one of the dormitory walls when I visited.

Like those children, we can look at the hole under the tree and play with something that seems gorgeous, until a situation brings out its true nature. Do you know what you really are on the inside? To find out, apply the law of God.

"What shall we say, then?" Paul asks.

Is the law sin? Certainly not! Indeed I would not have known what sin was except through the law. For I would not have known what coveting was if the law had not said, "Do not covet." But sin, seizing the opportunity afforded by the commandment, produced in me every kind of covetous desire.

Romans 7:7-8

Paul is telling us that within each of us lies the latent capacity for sin. Somehow we have to come to terms with our sinful capacity. A lot of us don't believe it's there, so something must be applied so that sin will reveal itself to us. The sin coils itself up inside us, and on the outside we're lovely people. Somehow or other God has to make it strike so we can know it for what it is.

The Ten Commandments make it strike. As we expose ourselves to them we discover how greedy we are; we discover how lustful we are; we discover how much we can become strangers to the truth, when it serves us. As we look at these and the other sins it has opened our eyes to, we ask, "Is that me?" The answer is, "Yes. That's the real me."

Nobody will keep the law, and we have to recognize our own sinfulness through the law, as God applies it to our lives.

## Made right with God

In Romans 8:3 we read, "What the law was powerless to do in that it was weakened by the sinful nature, God did." The law was powerless to make us right with God. The Ten Commandments cannot make anyone fit for heaven and cannot equip us to live as we ought because of the weakness of our sinful nature.

Now this does not mean there is something wrong with the law. It means there's something wrong with the material the law has to work with. Many years ago, when I went to high school, we had a teacher who came in to do choral music in our school. He had a tremendous reputation for producing marvelous choirs all around the area. Yet he left our school in utter despair. Why? Because there he found a bunch of kids who didn't like music or who didn't want to sing, even if they did like music, and every single one had a voice like a frog.

Now that's not to suggest our teacher was not a brilliant musician—he was. The material he had to work with caused the problem. The same is true of the Ten Commandments. They have to work with me and you. We have a sinful nature that remains apathetic toward God's law or is antagonistic toward it. Because of our nature and the holiness of God, we don't have what it takes when it comes to fulfilling the Ten Commandments.

Listen to the good news. What the law was powerless to do, God did. What did he do? He sent his Son, in the likeness of sinful man, to help man know God. And Jesus fulfilled the law. He was the Ten Commandments on two legs, living, breathing, warm, and magnificent. Now added to the law that condemns us, we have the life of Christ to condemn us. But Jesus didn't just come to do that. He went to the cross as a sin offering. All the consequences of the broken law, all the curse upon us for not being what we should, all the consequences of our sin nature coming to the fore and striking against the law and doing all manner of things wrong—God heaped those up, gathered them together, and placed them on Christ, who died for our sins.

Have you ever met anyone for whom Christ did not die? Have you met someone for whom his death did not blot out sin, cleansing him and making him right with God? The answer is no. That person has not been born and will not be born. We are the very people for whom Christ died, that we might be forgiven.

## A Change of Heart

Maybe you want to ask, "Hey, if the Ten Commandments can't save us, why bother studying them?" There's one final thing about the law.

The Ten Commandments show us our sin and lead us, ashamed, to Christ so that we might be forgiven, so that we can come alive through the Lord Jesus Christ who died for each of us. What does he do when he comes into my life? He writes his law on my heart. That means he changes my desires and my aspirations. He alters the direction of my life and gives me the power to change. As the living Christ comes into my life the righteousness of the law becomes fulfilled in me. First I find a new love for the Lord; I desire to have him. I have a new interest in the Lord's day and a new concern for others. As I see lust and greed for what they are, I turn from them. All those things that are sin begin to move away.

Because of the changes in my heart, I begin to demonstrate I'm walking in the law and fulfilling the righteousness of the law.

Once, on a plane, I had my Bible out, doing some catch-up reading. A stewardess came up and said, "Mustn't spill coffee on the good book, must we?"

"No, we mustn't," I responded.

Awhile later another one had a word with me, then stayed and we talked. She said, "You know, four years ago the Bible was a dead book to me. Then something happened, and I can't explain it, but I can't get enough of it. I devour it."

"I know what happened," I answered. "Have you ever read a book that was boring, then one day you met the author? Afterwards you picked up the same book and said, 'I know who wrote this,' and it became the most exciting book in the world to you."

"Yes, that's what happened to me. I met the author."

When you meet the author of the Word of God, he begins to write it in your heart instead of hitting you over the head with it. You begin to desire it instead of resenting it. You long to see it work out in your life, rather than saying, "Why does God say this to me?"

That change of heart shows you've repented of your sin, God has forgiven you, and the living Christ has come into your heart. Now the law of righteousness is fulfilled in you, because you walk after the Spirit, not after the flesh. As you go through life you increasingly become the Ten Commandments on two legs, living, breathing, moving, warm, demonstrating your love for the Lord and your love for other people. It becomes important to you.

As you've read, have you gone through the Commandments saying to yourself, "Hey, I kept that one"? Or did you say, "Yeah, I'm all right on this one," only to discover later, "Uh-ho, he got me!" Did you notice that bit by bit you found different things you'd slipped up on? Well, that wasn't the point.

The point is that as we expose ourselves to the law and keep it—which we haven't done—we begin to understand that by it no one will be made righteous. In addition we start to discover the sinfulness of our own sinful nature. Does that bother you? Did you begin to say, "O God, what on earth can I do?"

God says, "Nothing. I've done it. I've given Christ as a sin offering for you. Now you know your sin. You know the impossibility of getting rid of it. But listen up. I have taken your sin and placed it on Christ. He did it for you. If you will come to him and acknowledge what you are and ask him to forgive you and invite him to come and change your heart, your mind, and your life, he will."

As you look at your life, can you say, "That's what I was, and this is what I am"? Can you say, "The law showed me my sin and led me to Christ. I was forgiven. The living Christ came into my life by his Spirit and changed me. Now I have an overriding desire to live his way"? If so, you'll know you're different.

If that hasn't happened, it sure needs to, because if it doesn't, your sporadic efforts at keeping the law will no more fit you for earth than they will help you into heaven. Here your feeble efforts will seem pretty useless while they won't do a thing at all to right things with God. Only God can change your spirit when you come to him in repentance. Half-hearted efforts to keep the Commandments won't open the way to eternal life.

Where are you today? Do you need to make a first commitment to God? If the answer is yes, why not take time to do so now? Or do you have a commitment to him that has gotten a bit fuzzy or frayed around the edges? Use this chance to review what God has done for you. Spend some time with him in prayer and get things straightened out.

Then take time out to learn what it means to play by the rules!

# Suggested Reading

Anderson, Norman. *Issues of Life and Death*. Downers Grove, Ill.: Inter-Varsity Press, 1977.

Barclay, William. *The Ten Commandments for Today*. New York: Harper & Row, 1983.

Bernbaum, John A., ed. *Perspectives on Peacemaking*. Ventura, Calif.: Regal Books, 1984.

Carson, D. A. *From Sabbath to Lord's Day*. Grand Rapids, Mich.: Zondervan, 1982.

Catherwood, Frederick. *First Things First*. Downers Grove, Ill.: InterVarsity Press, 1979.

Clouse, Robert G., ed. *War*. Downers Grove, Ill.: InterVarsity Press, 1981.

Davidman, Joy. *Smoke on the Mountain*. Philadelphia: Westminster Press, 1953.

Gardner, R. F. R. *Abortion*. Exeter: Paternoster Press, 1972.

Geisler, Norman L. *Ethics: Alternatives and Issues*. Grand Rapids, Mich.: Zondervan, 1971.

Goudzwaard, Bob. *Idols of Our Time*. Downers Grove, Ill.: InterVarsity Press, 1984.

Keye, Bruce and Gordon Wenham, eds. *Law, Morality and the Bible*. Downers Grove, Ill.: InterVarsity Press, 1978.

Mackay, Donald M. *Human Science and Human Dignity*, Downers Grove, Ill.: InterVarsity Press, 1979.

Palmer, Earl F. *Old Law—New Life*. Nashville, Tenn.: Abingdon Press, 1984.

Schlossberg, Herbert. *Idols for Destruction*. Nashville, Tenn.: Thomas Nelson, 1982.

Watson, Thomas. *The Ten Commandments*. Edinburgh: Banner of Truth Trust, 1965.

# Foundations of the Faith

## Stuart Briscoe

### The Fruit of the Spirit
### Cultivating Christian Character

The author helps us to examine and meditate on
the qualities of character listed in Galatians 5:22–
3, demonstrating that the fruit of the Spirit is not
merely a collection of gifts from which we can
pick and choose, but rather a description of
Christian behaviour as it is meant to be.

ISBN 1-85078-144-3

### The Apostles' Creed
### Beliefs that Matter

With his characteristic wit and candour, Stuart
Briscoe studies each phrase of the Apostles'
Creed, bringing to life the foundational truths of
the Christian faith concerning the Father, the
Son, the Holy Spirit, the Church, sin and
salvation, and eternal life.

ISBN 1-85078-171-0

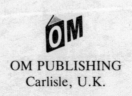

OM PUBLISHING
Carlisle, U.K.

# Back to Basics
## The Anatomy of a Slogan

## David Porter

With a foreword by David Alton MP

Despite the collapse of the 'Back to Basics'
campaign, many wish that the slogan could have
meant more than the aimless charade that it
became. John Major did touch a deep chord in the
nation.

'In this highly readable book, David Porter spells
out the real meaning of "Back to Basics".
Challenging to politicians of all faiths, it is
essential reading for Christians committed to
citizenship of both Kingdom and world.'

—*Martyn Eden, **Evangelical Alliance***

'What has been missing so far in the "Back to
Basics" debate, and what David Porter provides
in this book, is the balanced approach of Christian
ethics.'

—*David Alton MP*

ISBN 1-85078-155-9

OM PUBLISHING
Carlisle, U.K.

# Restoring the Image

## Roger Hurding

Amidst the plethora of books on counselling, here is a clear treatment of the subject for the non-specialist, covering every aspect of life, including adolescence, singleness, early years of marriage, as well as divorce and bereavement.

'Unlike many books on counselling [this] is free from the psychiatric and theological jargon guaranteed to send the reader into reverse gear . . . This is readable.'

—*Ann Townsend*, **Life of Faith**

'Well presented, psychologically authentic and scriptural.'

—**Churchman**

ISBN 1-85078-138-9

OM PUBLISHING
Carlisle, U.K.

# Passion and Purity
## How to Bring Your Love Life under Christ's Control

## Elisabeth Elliot

'Warmly personal . . . *Passion and Purity*
couldn't be more timely, more on target.'
—*Ruth Bell Graham*

'This book is definitely for men too'
—*Billy Graham*

Through letters, diary entries and recollections of
her courtship and marriage to Jim Elliot, his
widow candidly shares the temptations,
difficulties, victories and sacrifices of two young
people whose commitment to Christ took priority
over their love for each other.

Revealing personal glimpses, combined with
relevant biblical teaching, provide realistic
guidance in today's climate of confused and
compromising moral standards. Areas covered
include dating, singleness or marriage, virginity
and chastity, men and women's roles, and
putting God first in relationships

ISBN 1-85078-147-8

OM PUBLISHING
Carlisle, U.K.

# Three Crucial Questions about Jesus

## Murray J. Harris

The author provides in creatively different ways a triple defence of the validity of Christianity.

Did Jesus Exist?

A survey of four classical writers for evidence that a person named Jesus of Nazareth lived in Israel in the first century.

Did Jesus Rise from the Dead?

In the form of a debate, objections are examined including the swoon theory, alternative explanations for the empty tomb, psychological explanations for the recorded appearances, and the Turin Shroud.

Is Jesus God?

Harris amasses the New Testament evidence that teaches that Jesus is God and discusses his divine status, divine functions and use of the title 'God'.

ISBN 1-85078-137-0

OM PUBLISHING
Carlisle, U.K.

# OM PUBLISHING

OM Publishing specializes in popular paperbacks in three vital areas of the church's work:

EVANGELISM
DISCIPLESHIP
MISSION

In addition, OM Publishing spearheaded the 'Pray for the World' campaign, led by the titles *Operation World* and *You Can Change the World*.

For a free catalogue, write now to:

OM Publishing, PO Box 300, Carlisle, Cumbria CA3 0QS, UK.

OM PUBLISHING
Carlisle, U.K.